Learning by Teaching

This book provides an essential overview of "learning by teaching", unpacking the underpinning theory, research evidence and practical implications of peer learning in a variety of classroom contexts.

It aims to offer practical guidance for practitioners in structuring effective peer learning – between professionals and between students alike. It locates this phenomenon in current conceptions of learning and teaching, far removed from traditional ideas of one-way transmission of knowledge. Exactly what happens to promote learning by teaching is explored. Examples of learning by teaching are discussed and it is noted that this happens in school, university and the workplace, as well as through the Internet. Learning by teaching within the student body is then explored, and many different methods described. The organizational features needed to improve learning by teaching consciously and deliberately are investigated. These can be before teaching, during teaching or after teaching. Evidence-based practical guidance is given.

Of course teachers can deploy learning by teaching for themselves, but what if they also organize their students to teach each other, thereby giving many more opportunities to discuss, practise, explain and question? This takes pedagogical advantage of the differences between students – turning classrooms into communities of learners where students learn both from their teacher and from their peers.

David Duran is Assistant Professor of Educational Psychology at the Autonomous University of Barcelona, Spain. David previously worked for over 15 years as a secondary school teacher, before moving on to initial teacher training, and co-ordinating the Research Group on Peer Learning (GRAI), which trains teachers and schools to implement programmes based on peer tutoring.

Keith Topping is Professor of Educational and Social Research in the School of Education, University of Dundee, UK, where he is also Director of the Centre for Peer Learning. Having previously worked as a teacher, social worker, health specialist and educational advisor, Keith's interest now lies with peer learning, and he has advised national governments and organizations on the topic.

Learning by Teaching

Evidence-based Strategies to Enhance Learning in the Classroom

David Duran and Keith Topping

Routledge
Taylor & Francis Group

LONDON AND NEW YORK

First published 2017
by Routledge
2 Park Square, Milton Park, Abingdon, Oxon OX14 4RN

and by Routledge
711 Third Avenue, New York, NY 10017

Routledge is an imprint of the Taylor & Francis Group, an informa business

Part of this book is based on Duran, D. (2014). *Aprenseñar. Evidencias e implicaciones educativas de aprender enseñando.* Madrid: Narcea.

British Library Cataloguing in Publication Data
A catalogue record for this book is available from the British Library

Library of Congress Cataloging in Publication Data
Names: Duran, David, author. | Topping, Keith J., author.
Title: Learning by teaching : evidence-based strategies to enhance learning in the classroom / David Duran and Keith Topping.
Description: Abingdon, Oxon ; New York, NY : Routledge is an imprint of the Taylor & Francis Group, an Informa Business, [2017] | Includes bibliographical references.
Identifiers: LCCN 2016044664| ISBN 9781138122987 (hbk) |
ISBN 9781138122994 (pbk) | ISBN 9781315649047 (ebk)
Subjects: LCSH: Reflective teaching. | Learning.
Classification: LCC LB1025.3 .D86 2017 | DDC 371.102—dc23
LC record available at https://lccn.loc.gov/2016044664

ISBN: 978-1-138-12298-7 (hbk)
ISBN: 978-1-138-12299-4 (pbk)
ISBN: 978-1-315-64904-7 (ebk)

Typeset in Times New Roman
by diacriTech, Chennai

MIX
Paper from
responsible sources
FSC
www.fsc.org   FSC® C013056

Printed and bound in Great Britain by
TJ International Ltd, Padstow, Cornwall

Contents

Acknowledgement

Part of this book is based on Duran, D. (2014). *Aprenseñar. Evidencias e implicaciones educativas de aprender enseñando*. Madrid: Narcea.

Chapter 1

Learning by teaching

A new game of words?

Who teaches learns by teaching and who learns teaches by learning.

Paulo Freire (1996: p16)

We all have experiences of having learned something by teaching it

Learning requires effort. And learning occupies room. Perhaps that is the reason why our minds, cleverly, tend to learn only what they find interesting or necessary. But in addition, the format of teaching, the format of presenting information and especially the requirements of participation can facilitate or hinder the learning – even when it interests us.

Many times we have taken a plane, and we know that flying is an activity that involves some risk. The airline companies provide us with an explanation about security measures – the crew members planted before us perform a liturgy with vests and emergency exits. There is no doubt that what they say could be vital. That is why companies use all their means to explain security measures.

Of course some may think that if one day the pilot announces that the plane will crash, the best option will be praying. What little will the vest do, when we do not even fly over any sea? But, in reality, we know that aircraft are safe and that such a risk is not very great.

Despite having heard such information so many times, do we know what to do if the plane suffers a depressurization? Do we have a rapid response? If that occurs, are we able to remain calm and put on the oxygen mask in fifteen seconds? If we can, we will arrive (somewhat dishevelled, of course) at an airport. If we can't, we will lose consciousness and put our lives at risk.

This is a simple example about something that is vitally important about learning, which, however, we often do not learn. Being subject to explanations – texts (in brochures), orally (via speakers), kinetically (with representation or demonstration) or through video (trying to combine all this) – is not always effective.

Years ago a teacher, talking about the theme of this book, said: "Imagine an alternative – instead, as you're entering the plane the stewardess says: 'It's your turn!' Then she asks you to teach the security measures to the rest of the passengers. In the time before takeoff, with their help and resources, you have mastered the task perfectly. The crew ensured that the passenger explainers understand it exactly".

This is not just a suggestion to the airline companies, since there are already enough requirements about flying. It is more a prompt to encourage you to reflect on the times when you have learned things through having to explain them to others. Shortly we will discuss some research (Cortese, 2005) which shows that professionals from different fields admit that their maximum learning moments have much to do with real work experiences in which they have had to teach something to a less experienced person. We will see how formal education accepts this principle and, for example, medical students at the University of São Paulo learn to teach first aid to ordinary citizens. These future doctors learn it much better than if it was just explained to them (Fraga, Caravalho, Hirano & Bollela, 2012).

Have you ever learned the name of a street in your city by helping someone to find it? Your knowledge of the environment, the tourist's map and the tourist's request allow you to learn. Following that thread, we often take advantage of friends coming from other places to learn about our own environment, when we have to present it to them. Being a tourist friend and guide offers us opportunities to know places better (landscapes, tourist places, museums, etc.) and investigate human activities which, despite the geographical proximity, were formerly little known to us.

These ways of learning by teaching others have been multiplied by the Internet. In many forums and websites of the Internet there are people learning (e.g. they inform, they solve problems) in order to help others. Peer-to-peer (P2P) proposals are based on the idea of learning from one another, including the possibility that the experts also learn by teaching people who are less expert or who have requested their help. Take, for example, the video tutorials to show you how to play the guitar. When someone distributes one of those videos, even without knowing if anyone will use it, we can be sure that the creator has truly learned to play the tunes in order to teach others how to play them. We will see later how schools can motivate students to make a tutorial video for others, as a mechanism for the creator's learning: a process of learning by teaching.

It is not hard to find episodes in our lives where we have learned by teaching others. Perhaps that is the reason why famous historical teachers have left us testimony to that effect:

- "Teaching is learning" (Seneca [4 BC–AD 65]).
- "Who teaches others, learns himself" (Comenius [1592–1670]).
- "To teach is to learn twice" (Joubert [1754–1824]).
- "For me, there is no separation between teaching and learning, because when you teach you also learn" (Casals [1876–1973]).

As we shall see in Chapter 2, the activity of teaching, which is exclusively human, requires us to take part in social processes where tutors can participate in the learning that they aim to develop in others.

Is there scientific evidence that teaching is a way of learning?

It seems that there are experiences across times and cultures that testify that teaching others can be a good way to learn. The "pyramid of learning" indicates that teaching is the best way to learn, and it is attributed to the National Training Laboratories in Bethel, Maine, in the United States. This holds that trainees retain

- 90 per cent of what you learn when you teach it to others,
- 75 per cent of what you learn when you practise it,
- 50 per cent of what you learn through a group discussion,
- 30 per cent of what you learn through a demonstration,
- 20 per cent of what you learn through audio-visual means,
- 10 per cent of what you learn through reading, and
- 5 per cent of what you learn through formal instruction.

The curious thing is that such research does not exist. The use and dissemination of such a pyramid reflects only intuition and experience which makes us think. Probably, this pyramid is inspired by the "cone of experience" of Edgar Dale (1946), who argues that the retention of studied material is based on the level of involvement or activity that we deploy as we learn. Thus, effective ways of learning overcome passivity (e.g. read, hear, see) and require action and interaction (e.g. talk, discuss, represent, simulate or make). This approach also helped the introduction of the concept of "learning by doing", which affirmed the importance of procedures over factual or conceptual knowledge.

Without a doubt, teaching others involves an active role from the tutor. However, asserting that this is the most effective way of learning requires investigation of the scientific knowledge available. Fortunately, we have research that endorses these experiences – that learning by teaching is possible. Chapter 3 reviews such research, noting that the role of tutor has many variations (e.g. supervisor, instructor, trainer, tutor, teacher, mentor) but always meets the condition of offering learning opportunities to the person who plays it. In addition, there are numerous practices in informal education, both in face-to-face and virtual contexts, emphasizing the potential of learning by teaching. Given the importance and effectiveness of this type of learning, Chapter 4 will address these practices and will try to draw some lessons for formal education.

What do teachers think of all this?

Some years ago we asked education professionals – teachers in primary and secondary schools and university – about their perspective of peer learning, from their own experience. When we asked them to indicate if they had experiences of having learned themselves by teaching their students, every one raised their hand. Later we found this was true for teachers of different educational stages and different geographical contexts. Delving into the reasons for such results, teachers seem to report three types of reasons.

The first has to do with the opportunities offered by the practice of teaching to improve teaching competence. *Learning through exercising the profession*, as one teacher put it. Following concepts based on the importance of practice and professional experience, these teachers suggested that professional practice (teaching) allowed them the possibility of teacher improvement (learning). This math teacher put it clearly:

> *And that is the beauty of teaching: in fact, it is learning by the teacher; we learn as much as they. While children learn new skills and new mathematical concepts, we learn to create appropriate learning situations, learn to carefully observe the processes that take place in them and learn to correct to help our children whenever they needed it.*
>
> (http://aprendiendomatematicas.com/aprender-ensenando/
> Malena Martín, retrieved 8 December 2016)

A second group of teachers reported experiences in which they themselves had to learn what they had then to teach their students. We could call this "learning to teach". The most powerful experiences here are linked to unexpected questions from the students. A high school teacher commented:

> *I remember that I learned a lot of contemporary history when I had to teach the subject to high school students. Before each class, it was me who was brooding over the text book and performing all the activities… preparing schema … I learned a lot!*

Some teachers used methodologies that allowed them to "learn while they teach". In this way, they were open to the interests of students and helped turn these questions into learning objectives which were achieved through an open process of teamwork, with the participation of the community. A primary school teacher talked about his work for projects or research groups:

> *I don't place myself in front of my students, but at their side in the process of learning to undertake. All together, we make questions, generate projects and I accompany them on the journey of learning. I try to learn with them. In addition to the information available on the network, on a regular basis we invite families, or experts on issues.*

In one way or another, the experience of learning by teaching is nothing strange for education professionals. However, sometimes this leads to something more profound and thoughtful – experiences that go in the opposite direction. We could call this "teaching to unlearn". A university professor exemplified it:

> *I remember the first few times, when I was preparing themes, I learned it myself. But then, as the years have passed, I think that I have been "slimming" contents, making them more schematic and I have the feeling that I know less than before.*

And the certainties are that in my classes those who learn are, of course, students, I only teach them.

It seems that the practical knowledge of teachers brings us something that the research also says: it is not *always* the case that teaching offers learning opportunities for those who teach. Two factors are relevant here.

First, the conception that the teacher has of what teaching and learning is can be crucially important, and the biases or attitudes derived from this. If the teacher has an archaic concept of teaching, seeing their role as simply to transmit information already known by them, they will hardly learn (by teaching). The ancient conception in which the teacher is the (only) one who teaches and the student is the (only) one who learns is well established in the context of formal education and leads some to resist any change. Let us give an example from the perspective of students. For years, our research groups piloted several programs of peer tutoring, through which more competent students learn to teach peers with fewer skills. Despite having empirical evidence of this (for instance, Duran & Monereo, 2008), when we asked peer tutors if they learned, many tended to reproduce the predominant cultural conception and said those who learned were the peer tutees. The conception of learning and teaching thus plays an important role in the possibilities for learning by teaching. We will discuss this further in Chapter 2.

Second, the methodologies adopted by teachers to some extent determine the learning opportunities that teaching holds for them. As we will see in the findings of research in the field, moving away from one-way forms of instruction (e.g. directive, rote, transmissive) to make use of methodologies that promote bidirectionality (encouraging students to interact, ask, suggest topics, etc.), as well as the reflective construction of knowledge from explanations and questions, will promote learning opportunities for those who develop the role of tutor.

If we are able to counter these two features with a more current and evidence-based concept, recognizing the conditions that limit or enhance the tutor's learning, we will be able to facilitate the extension of peer-led educational practices that are breaking through in the fields of formal and informal education. In Chapter 5 we will outline methodologies and experiences based on learning by teaching: practices of peer tutoring as already mentioned; cooperative learning methods that promote deliberate episodes in which students learn to teach the rest of their teammates; students who make teaching artefacts (such as instructional videos) so that others can learn what they have already learned; experiences of peer assessment in which students learn by editing others' work, reflecting and offering feedback; and many others.

Such practices, some of them still considered innovations, allow students to learn to teach and teach to learn. Perhaps teaching to learn is one of the emerging skills we need for twenty-first-century citizenship. In our learning and knowledge society that calls upon us to learn throughout our lives, learning to learn seems insufficient. Competences need to be generalized across many contexts.

If all learning came only from teaching, we would need a very substantial part of the workforce dedicated to teaching professionally. That seems very unrealistic.

Would not this lead to an even more unequal society, where only those with economic resources could access continuing training? It seems that we will have to learn and teach daily, by learning from one another. How, then, will we build a democratic, lifelong learning society?

Finally, we will close the book with Chapter 6, where we sum up that education professionals should teach by learning themselves. If we can do this – if we ourselves learn about what we teach – not only will we constantly update our knowledge (something that is very valuable in a changing society), but also we will surely live with more interest and improve our profession.

Chapter 2

Teaching and learning in the age of knowledge

What makes us human is cooperation.

Michael Tomasello (2009: p157)

The conception we have about what teaching and learning is will have direct consequences on our predisposition to learning by teaching, either as a teacher or as a learner. If in our minds remains the traditional idea of teaching as a transfer of information from the mind of the teacher to that of the student, we can hardly design situations in which we give our students opportunities to learn from one another, or contexts in which we can learn with and from them.

This chapter will review the role of culture in the development of teaching and learning, particularly changes in conceptions of teaching and learning in the knowledge society and the conceptual implications that learning and teaching have. When we talk about learning, we can think of it as learning in three dimensions (length, width and depth) – and this chapter is structured in this way.

Teaching and learning in our species

Learning is not exclusively human. All animals learn. As Steven Pinker (1997) explains, the ability to learn appeared in some ancestor of multicellular animals and probably guided the evolution of nervous systems towards the specialization of neuronal circuits.

However, the idea that animals learn – or are "trained" – by associating a stimulus with a response through rewards or punishments is limited to larger organisms. The sophisticated guidance systems that ants use to return to their nests and migratory birds use to travel are examples of the execution of complex sequences of data processing with complicated arithmetic and logical operations, which demonstrate that each species has developed machinery (in brain and body) to solve their own problems. The brain is a high-precision instrument that allows each creature to use information to solve problems posed by their way of life.

Now, don't ask the stork how it does it. Sophisticated navigation calculations occur in the brain unconsciously. Instinctively. Default mechanisms, inherited by the species, provide guidelines of conduct. These unconsciously use information and decision-making processes to solve problems. We also have these – we act instinctively, we learn implicitly. But our evolutionary path, rather than specializing our brain as a problem-solving device, has sought to avoid devices that act as a mental replacement part and can be used more flexibly.

According to Pinker, the brains of humans retain similarities with those of mammals and primates, but differs from them, both quantitatively (by its large size in relation to the rest of the body, continuing to grow after birth) and qualitatively (allowing the combination of neural circuits). These are exclusively human characteristics, which differentiate us from the great apes, such as bipedalism, increased life expectancy and widespread breeding of new members. The evolutionary aspects that have led us to that "cognitive niche" in evolution are related to different elements:

- Having a good visual system, in three dimensions and full colour, which has allowed us to develop abstraction.
- Living in groups, which favours having more information (benefitting from it or having to negotiate with it) and, in turn, promotes new cognitive challenges.
- Having hands, released by bipedalism, able to carry objects and manipulate them with much precision, creating and transforming tools.
- Hunting, which has allowed us to develop working in teams and social intelligence (not only for capturing larger prey, but also to socially share the spoils). Adding meat in the diet has given us the nutrients to develop our brains and expand into every corner of the planet, even in those areas where grass does not grow.

In short, what in the eyes of the evolutionary psychologists seems responsible for our makeup as a species – what makes us smarter than chimpanzees – is that human intelligence is not the result of only individual effort. Cooperation – working with others – has played a crucial role in the development of our species. It has allowed us to accumulate knowledge and skills to share among individuals and across generations. Albert Einstein (1879–1955), one of the best known and most significant names of the twentieth century, wrote:

> *A hundred times every day I remind myself that my inner and outer life depend on the labours of other men, living and dead, and that I must exert myself in order to give in the same measure as I have received and am still receiving.*
>
> (Einstein, 1949, p. 3)

This is what Tomasello (2009), from the cognitive sciences, called cumulative cultural evolution. Each of us not only inherits genes, which involved adjustments in the past, but also inherits, through culture, artefacts and behavioural practices that represent the collective wisdom of our ancestors. Thus, we have inherited genes and memes. This last term (Dawkins, 1976) makes reference to the transmission of behaviours along generations. There is no other animal species which accumulates behavioural changes and ensures their complexity with this kind of device.

According to Tomasello, the second characteristic that is unique to human culture is the creation of social institutions (practically guided by different types of rules and regulations that individuals recognize for each other). Thus, for example, in all cultures individuals adhere to certain cultural rules to mate and live together; to share food or valuables and sell them; or to recognize group leaders. After those two characteristics of human culture – cumulative artefacts and social institutions – there is a set of cooperative skills and motivations to collaborate that are unique to our species.

Tomasello, Hare, Lehmann and Call (2007) have formulated the "cooperative eye hypothesis", which suggests that the human eye reveals the direction of the look, thanks to a large sclera, more than any of 200 species of primates has. This allows cooperation, through mutual observation of the focus of attention. The cooperative eye is an evolutionary product of a social environment in which disclosure of information is beneficial. These skills and motivations are based on joint attention and mutual knowledge and are embodied in three processes:

1   Imitative learning, whose intrinsic characteristic is not cooperation but use. Advances in neuroscience (and especially in the field of neurons) (Iacaboni, 2008) show that even though imitative behaviours are shared with other species, learning by imitation – i.e. the ability to learn through observation – is limited to humans and perhaps the great apes.
2   Education. Humans teach each other different things, not just in the nursing period (as for other species). Teaching is a form of altruism in which we provide information to others so that they use it. As we shall see in more detail in the next chapter, learning is not exclusively human, but teaching is.
3   Conformation to the group. We tend to imitate other individuals of the group we associate with, not clash with them. We are created so that our personality and the identity of the group are complementary, developing also social compliance standards. Harris (1999) reviews research in evolutionary psychology and proposes taking into account the influence of the peer group in the socialization of the individual, above that of the family and adults.

Research has compiled evidence of all this through comparative studies of different species and studies on the development of evolution. Comparative studies between species have mainly focused on the contrast between human children and chimpanzees (Warneken, Chen & Tomasello, 2006). Thus, from nine months of age babies develop initiatives to share attention with others, through a "triangle" that arises when they begin to point out objects for joint action with other significant family and friends. In various experiments, children aged 18–24 months and young chimpanzees interacted in four cooperative activities with an adult human partner. Children participated successfully in the resolution of problems in cooperative and social games, while chimpanzees were only interested in social games. When the adult partner stopped participating in the midst of the activity, all the children produced at least one communication attempt, trying to restore the shared process. On the other hand, no chimpanzee tried to regain joint activity. Children not only try to communicate to establish acts of cooperation from nine months, but also they share and cooperate simply for pleasure, when they don't need it.

The evidence provided by studies of human development are very extensive and agree that already in the first year of life children manifest an innate inclination to cooperate. For the first three years, this is affected by expectations of reciprocity (tending to help those who also help us); by the view of the group (reputation and public self); and by the view of punishment and social norms (which we learn and enforce, just as in the *ultimatum game*, for example). The *ultimatum game* is one of many experiments deriving from the theory of games that allow us to analyse human behaviour. In this game with two players, the experimenter offers the first player a sum of money. The first player proposes to the second how to divide this sum between them. The second player chooses either to accept or reject this offer. If the second player accepts, the money is split according to the proposal. If the second player rejects the offer, neither player receives any money. Multiple repetitions of this experiment indicate that people from different origins and conditions tend to reject offerings below 30 per cent. We prefer justice (and not winning anything) to a benefit considered unfair.

Harris (2006) offers a very suggestive theory of the functioning of the human mind, establishing three systems that act in combination: the relational (which helps us to establish and maintain relationships with others), the socializing (which helps us to become a member of the group) and status (which drives us to try to be better than our rivals).

Humans, unlike other species such as chimpanzees, have sophisticated tools to share emotional or psychological states with others. One of them is what has been called the "theory of mind" or the capacity to read the mind of the other (Baron-Cohen, Leslie & Frith, 1985). This concept, originally used in primatology and autism studies, allows us to understand how we explain and predict the behaviour of others.

Let's see what we're talking about through the popular test of Anne and Sally (or the false belief). This shows two dolls, Sally and Anne, representing a small scene for children: Sally has a basket and Anne a box. Sally has a marble and put it in her basket. Then she leaves, disappearing from the scene. While Sally is out, Anne takes the marble from the basket and saves it in the box. Then Sally returns and wants to play with her marble. At that time the child asks: *Where will Sally look for her marble?* Except for people with autism, children of four years are usually able to properly answer this question, responding "in the basket"; that is, they are able to represent in their mind the state of knowledge of Sally – who does not know that the marble is not in her basket, because she has not seen the change – even when the state of knowledge of the observing child is different. We can represent to ourselves, not the reality, but the reality of the mind of others.

Juan Ignacio Pozo (2006) writes that our capacity not only to know what we know and, therefore, what we ignore, but also to imagine or guess what others know or ignore – these features show our meta-representational capacity. It seems to be a specifically human trait that is part of our cognitive identity as *homo sapiens sapiens* ("the man who knows he knows").

The second tool that allows us to share mental states with others is language. With only a word, we can change the mind of others. Simply writing "omelette", we are generating a representation in our mind. And this is also shared. Language allows the construction of knowledge together with others and, in its written form or through other existing forms of representation (e.g. voice recordings, audiovisual) facilitates the construction of knowledge through the generations.

Changes in the conceptions of teaching and learning

As we have seen, our species has made an evolutionary path that combines biological heritage – through genes that predispose us to develop human capacities – with cultural heritage, resulting from accumulating and refining valid knowledge to solve social problems.

That cultural inheritance, which separates us from the rest of the animals, requires us not only to generate culture, but to pass it on to the new citizens, something that we have seen that we do through complex mechanisms of cooperation that allow social practices of teaching and learning.

The nature of such practices has been very much mediated by the ways in which its participants understand what teaching and learning is – their representations – and also by the impact of the representation systems and technologies of knowledge, in each historical moment, to format our minds.

Learning and teaching: the same thing?

But prior to identifying some of the changes there have been in the concepts of teaching and learning, it should be remembered that the verbs "to teach" and "to learn" are not always conjugated together. Without calling into question the current trend in educational psychology to approach the study of the processes of teaching and learning as a whole – that one is not understood and explained without the other – it is also true that there are experiences of one without the other.

The ability to meta-represent what we have as humans (knowing what we know and what we ignore) allows us to guide our own learning. It allows us to be active learners on a permanent basis, from the moment of birth, and what is most interesting, learn of situations without being exposed to teaching (which can be defined as social activities designed deliberately to make someone learn something).

When babies learn to associate the figure of the mother with their welfare, or cry to get something or communicate with each other, they are not under a deliberate process of teaching; they do not intend to learn. Many of our everyday learnings occur in an incidental way, without requiring a purpose of deliberate learning and an awareness of what is being learned.

Our lives are filled with situations that offer us opportunities for our mind to learn: through participation in social situations (family, friends, media … or simply listening to a conversation on the bus) or through participation in non-formal support environments (museums, reports, affinity groups, or any of the multiple ways that the Internet offers) (Lacasa, 1994).

This knowledge, a product of situations where there is no deliberate teaching, is called implicit learning (Karmiloff-Smith, 1992) and we use it in different contexts without being aware of it. In fact, although implicit learning supports certain degrees of explication (to become accessible, consciously, to be able to be restructured), its essential characteristic is that it is not accessible to the consciousness of the subject and is, therefore, impenetrable (Pozo, 2001). The detection of regularities in our environment (our implicit knowledge) can become authentic theories in diverse domains (e.g. nature, society, relationships), which, although we cannot explain them (because of their implicitness), influence the way in which we behave and learn (Scheuer, Pozo, Pérez Echeverría, Mateos, Ortega & de la Cruz, 2006).

As teachers know, students come to school with much prior knowledge, which it is necessary to take into consideration to try to turn it into explicit knowledge. This can thus help to modify or improve the prior knowledge. Such knowledge, in the majority of cases, represents implicit learning, with a coherence from the point of view of the student (although not necessarily of science) and which can be shared with other people (when the prior knowledge is transmitted socially). But also, adults organize the world through implicit theories. "For example, all teaching is based on a conception of learning, more often implied and incidental, when who is now a teacher was then immersed, as an apprentice, in a certain culture of learning" (Pozo, 1996, p71). This is why we should be sharply aware of our incidental prior learning, in order to improve it.

We have said that there may be learning without teaching. And we must add that there is also teaching without learning. Although, perhaps, if the purpose of teaching is that someone learns, we should question if such activity was truly teaching. Perhaps inside of teaching it is possible that the student does not learn, as occurs in medical action, where unfortunately the sick are not always healed.

Not all social situations deliberately designed to help learning produce this effect. Of course. As students we have too often witnessed classes which did not ask us what we already knew of the issue, or what was interesting to us that we would like to deepen, or even what we did not understand. Much instruction was based on the passive position of the student, who received – a container to be filled – the information from the teacher. The teacher "gave" information to the class and it was assumed that the students turned it into knowledge. Much to assume.

John Dewey (1916), the famous American pedagogue, said that by "providing information" the students learn as if a car salesman had said: "I sold the car, but the customer did not buy it". As the sociologist Rafael Feito (2006, p104) rightly says: "A seller of this type, unlike what happens with teachers, would be increasing unemployment figures".

Today, we know that formats of transmissive and unidirectional learning are rarely effective. And the saddest thing, as we shall see below, is that this has been the major type of teaching in formal education.

The evolution of teaching and learning

The sociologist of education Mariano Fernández Enguita (2002) gives us an overview of socio-educational changes. We will present it here in a very schematic way (Table 2.1).

Societies prior to the industrial revolution – think for a moment of agriculture and livestock – were characterized by slowness of the pace of social change, in predictable and stable social scenarios. Changes, in general, occurred over generations, and it was not uncommon to start companies that concluded several generations later. Education and training took place in the bosom of families, where children often pursued the occupations of the parents; and members of the community used their experience when acting as instructors.

The new society, which emerged from the industrial revolution, speeded up the tempo of the social changes that occurred as a result of a society divided into classes with conflicting interests and a technology that accelerated what came to be called progress. Changes occurred between generations, between parents and children, with clashes of interests and values in the bosom of the family. It was in this social framework that the graduate school appeared that we know today; an instrument capable of transmitting the new work culture and the newly released forms of life. The need to adapt to the life of the factory, new rhythms, newly arrived forms of work and other elements that would mediate and influence the life of people from that time (for example, the clock) – these became the most effective agents for this new form of socialization (García-Lastra, 2013).

Table 2.1 Socio-educational changes

	Pre-industrial	Industrial	Knowledge
Life spent in a world…	Known, invariably	Different from the parents	In constant change
Perception	Stability, cyclical time	Crisis, progress and history	Uncertainty
Exchange rate	Supra-generational	Intergenerational	Intra-generational (inter in favour of young people)
Educational institution	Family, community	School	School, society
Educational agents	Elderly parents	Teachers	Teachers, peers
Base of educators	Experience	Initial training	Permanent training

Source: Adapted from Fernández Enguita, 2002.

Largely, the instruction and education of future generations were left in the hands of schools and professional teachers, who were trained before they began to teach. As in many other professions, in a social context where the workforce stayed stable enough, there was perhaps a little updating of knowledge acquired in school – or university, in the best of cases. Certainly enough to engage in their occupation throughout their working life. In that kind of society, adults – and among them professional teachers – had to transmit knowledge. The most important knowledge to transmit to new generations was what was necessary for them as citizens and workers. That is why schools taught content that students had to memorize to use out of school, in what Pablo Freire called transmissive pedagogy (Freire, 1984).

This fundamental idea of unilateral transmission of knowledge from the adult to the young person or child is based on a delivery model where the teacher holds the monopoly of knowledge and operates in the format "I teach – you learn".

The emergence of what has been called the knowledge society highlighted this mismatch and the obsolete conception of teaching and learning it embodied – with implications for the education system and schools. What seems to define today's society is change. As has been said many times, we are in a society characterized by change or in constant change. Probably because the tempo of social change has accelerated, the same generation can have many life experiences of change. Many of the activities we do on a daily basis (talking on a mobile phone or putting the air conditioning on in the car) were science fiction only a few decades ago. What we might be doing in a few years is unthinkable.

We live in an age where it seems that time has accelerated and the intervals between events are shortening. Not only does technology last for so little time and the computer becomes out-dated in a few months, but also the films, books, events – everything goes flying past. This rapid technological and social change accelerates and reduces the intervals of time between significant events. (Kurzweil, 1999).

Lamo de Espinosa (taken from Feito, 2006) highlights three essential knowledge society changes. First, the higher production of knowledge (the majority of scientists in the history of humanity are alive today). Second, science's gradual takeover of ordinary thinking (if before culture was science, science is now the dominant culture). Third, the greater social impact of knowledge (the time between basic knowledge production and product actualization and dissemination has lessened). According to Espinosa, the phone needed more than half a century between its discovery and its commercialization. The radio, 35 years. The radar, 15. Television, 10. The transistor, 15. How long did it take to commercialize the latest model of the smartphone?

This speed of change generates a perception of general uncertainty. In controversial and suggestive terms, Bauman (2000) calls society "liquid". Longworth (2003) writes, "We belong to the first generation that knows for sure that he does not know how it is going to be in the future" (p17). Fernández Enguita (2002) says that that we live in a society of intra-generational changes. Only a short life is required to undergo drastic changes; each of us will live through more and more striking social changes than would a vampire who lived for centuries.

In addition, within this society of intra-generational change, younger generations have more knowledge and skill than adults in certain domains, closely linked to the use of technologies of information and knowledge. For instance, a recent report (Ofcom, 2014) indicates that about half of parents of children aged 5 to 15 in the United Kingdom considered that their child knew more about the Internet than they did, as compared to 14 per cent of parents of children aged 3 to 4 years. These children or young people are part of the so-called native digital e-generation or net generation (Prensky, 2010), for which new media have formed an essential element in the process of socialization.

Educational systems in the knowledge society

All these elements have influenced the education system. Pozo, Scheuer, Pérez Echeverría, Mateos, Martín and de la Cruz (2006) argue that the knowledge society has generated a new culture of learning, characterized by the following:

- The school is no longer the first source of knowledge, and sometimes not even the main one. The students, like all of us, are bombarded by information, often excessively. More than simply providing information, schools should teach the ability to organize it, interpret it and provide it with some context, developing the students' skills so that they can transform information into knowledge and act upon it.
- We live in a society of multiple and uncertain knowledge. In this "age of uncertainty" (Morin, 2001), we must learn to live with a diversity of perspectives, theories and multiple interpretations of information relative to them, to build our own point of view.
- We are in a learning society. Much of the knowledge provided by the school is not only no longer absolute truth, but it has an expiration date. Even though we do not know what knowledge will be necessary for citizens of the next decade, what is indisputable is that they will have to learn both inside and outside the formal education system.

Faced with this situation, education systems have tried to respond to locate schools and educational institutions in a position more adjusted to the new reality. Some of the initiatives that have been taken in this direction are as follows:

1 Developing a broader conception of content than that on which the traditional school was based, introducing and underscoring the importance of procedures (know-how) and attitudes (savoir faire); allowing the student to overcome rote learning (essential only for factual content) by incorporating comprehensive learning (for concepts) and learning by doing (for procedures).
2 Proposing strategic or conditional learning (Pozo, Monereo & Castelló, 2001) and giving equal weight to the three types of knowledge: declarative, procedural and attitudinal. Strategic knowledge-based decision making is conscious

and reflective of its apprentice basis and the conditions which enable it (time and resources). For the teaching of learning strategies, Monereo, Pozo and Castelló propose a progressive transfer of control to the students, which would start with methods of explicit instruction (verbal instructions, cognitive modelling, analysis of cases of thought); guided practice, at a medium level of transfer (cumulated ideas on sheets of thought, discussion on the process of thinking, cooperative education) and autonomous practice (reciprocal teaching and peer tutoring).

3 Using metacognitive knowledge to manage or control how we use or deploy our own knowledge in the process of planning and evaluation of a task. Metacognition – the knowledge and control of the processes and mental activities related to the acquisition and use of knowledge – is closely linked to what has been termed "learning to learn" – essential for learning throughout life.

4 Training in competencies. We are unable to teach all skills, so we need to teach the ability to use knowledge and skills, in a transversal and interactive way, in contexts and situations that require knowledge linked to different knowledge, which implies understanding and using knowledge with awareness of the specific context. Perrenoud (2012) argues that compulsory school cannot claim to develop all the skills that a human being could possibly need someday, so it is essential to select those which are key. In this regard, there have been many interesting proposals, starting with the one provided by the Commission of UNESCO for education in the twenty-first century (UNESCO, 1996).

If the context of basic education (or compulsory education as some governments like to call it) has a necessarily limited role in the development of the skills required to function in the knowledge society, it is clear that these must be built permanently. John Seely Brown (Co-Chair of the Deloitte Center of Edge) argues that in the knowledge society, we need to connect *Homo sapiens* (knowledge), with *Homo faber* (know-how) and *Homo ludens* (enjoyment). This third component will play an essential role in learning in the new informal contexts of learning (Thomas & Seely Brown, 2011). The citizens of the knowledge society are damned – or perhaps winners – in learning long, wide and deep in our lives.

Although the idea of learning throughout our lives has already been sufficiently substantiated and can be synthesized – for example, by Cristóbal Cobo and John Moravec (2011) – do we need to abandon preventive knowledge? What is it that we learn throughout our lives? "Three-dimensional learning", "360-degree learning" and "24/7 learning" are terms that emphasize that learning takes place, ubiquitously, in formal spaces (schools that lead to accreditations or titles, for example), in non-formal spaces (such as refresher classes) and through informal learning (Longworth, 2003).

We have insisted on the importance of informal learning (through situations without educational intent) in the formation of knowledge and implicit theories which, although unconscious, guide our behaviour. How can formal education take into account the many ways in which in new knowledge is constructed? All of us have much more knowledge from informal learning than formal. Informal learning is highly effective, by the mere fact that learning continues beyond school and is often of an experiential nature. As Feito (2006, p15) says: "Real learning begins once school is abandoned".

For example, in the employment context, 80 per cent of learning comes from informal practices, and only 20 per cent is attributed to formal situations. Jay Cross, to whom is attributed the term "e-learning", argues that workers learn more in coffee time than in classrooms (Cross, 2006). This pre-eminence of informal learning has led some authors to represent formal learning as just the tip of the iceberg of what people know (Thomas & Seely Brown, 2011). The pedagogue Gimeno Sacristán (2012, p15) says that "the future of education will depend decisively on how we respond to the changes that are leading to the development of technologies of information out of the schools". While both types of knowledge are needed, as we have said, it seems advisable to situate the education system in the context of the knowledge society – to "informalize" the formal.

Miguel Angel Santos Guerra (another pedagogue) tells us how he proposes to his students that they respond to the hypothetical situation of how to organize a school of 500 students with a single teacher (Santos Guerra, 2012). The responses of students include innovative proposals of quality, such as the use of tutoring between students of different ages, the participation of the families and groupings based on activities and electronic media – proposals which, no doubt, bring us closer to informal learning experiences.

Information and communication technologies provide us with good environments to develop combined applications, enhancers of both formal and informal learning. A good example is the personal learning environments, jointing tools, sources of information, connections and activities that people use to learn (Castañeda & Adell, 2013). Many of these can be seen to be part of connectivism (Siemens, 2005), which proposes that what is important in today's society is not knowing *what*, or knowing *how*, but knowing *where* is the knowledge. In this theory, personal knowledge is formed from a network that feeds off information from organizations and institutions, which in turn feed back to such a network (such as on the Internet). Thus, learning becomes a kind of decision making, connecting nodes or information sources. Connectivism suggests that learners build connections by interests or needs, using technology.

In addition, we will have to learn intensively, not only always and everywhere. The concept of deep learning comes from sociocultural learning theory, derived from the contributions of the psychologist Lev Vygotsky, so called because of the social nature of culturally mediated human psychological processes. Vygotsky (1978) distinguishes between two lines of development: the natural, which corresponds to biologically scheduled deployment and includes psychological functions shared with animals; and the socio-cultural human, where higher psychological functions take place. The latter is where people are socialized through active participation in a community's specific culture. Interaction with other experts allows the appropriation of instruments and signs of culture, progressively increasing the possibilities of action of the participants.

The higher psychological processes also have their origin in social life, in interactions with others, through participating in culturally regulated activities. Through the "genetic law of cultural development", Vygotsky argues that any function appears twice: first, in a social or inter-psychological plane; and then, when a person internalizes it, on an intrapsychic or individual level. This "internalization" must be understood as a transformative process. The author uses the term "appropriation" to refer to this reconstruction which places the individual in an active role in the learning process. This internalization is made possible thanks to the interaction with experts (professors, peers, brothers) who share the knowledge and tools developed by the culture. As a result, learning is an activity performed by individuals in a social context and has its full realization in the creation of the socially oriented employment of artefacts to represent and broaden our understanding with and of each other (Wertsch, 1985).

Interactions involving learning take place in the Zone of Proximal Development (ZPD), which Vygotsky has defined as the space between the level of actual development (what you are capable of doing without the help of others) and the level of potential development (what you can do with help). Within the ZPD, the interaction offered by the mediators (who act between the mental activity of the apprentice and the new knowledge) becomes learning.

Education, understood as the support provided by the mediator in the ZPD, results in understanding, given the importance of the assistance provided to the student as well as the degree of adjustment and contingency. Mediators should offer the necessary minimum support and sequentially withdraw it from apprentices, who thereby make the learning their own.

This social and constructive conception of teaching and learning has been enriched by many contributions, such as the metaphor of scaffolded learning (Wood, Bruner & Ross, 1976), which implies dynamic support adjusting to the learning process; guided participation (Rogoff, 1990), which holds as the mediator builds bridges of actual to potential development, structures the involvement of the trainee and gradually transfers the control of the activity; and communities of practice (Lave & Wenger, 1991), which account for situated learning as a process that begins in legitimate peripheral participation and culminates in becoming an expert member of that community.

Teaching and learning through participation in the ZPD leads to an expanded conception of the zone (Wells, 1999) (which implies the opportunity of learning for all participants, including the mediator), and the possibility that the role of mediator (as more expert than the apprentice) can be developed for abler students, which gives rise to the notion that students can learn to teach each other. Both aspects will be revisited in the next chapter.

Here, keeping in mind the interaction with a mediator as a learning process moving towards increasingly deeper levels of knowledge, we would also like to refer to the spiral of knowledge, proposed by Gordon Wells. The spiral of knowledge is based on the different modes of knowledge that humanity has evolved: *instrumental* (prior to homo sapiens, based on the use of instruments to carry out activities); *procedural* (demonstrations or explanations of the use of instruments); *substantive* (reflections on conscious procedural knowledge and the increasingly complex nature of the activities led to having to choose between alternative means, depending on the conditions, and develop a generalized knowledge based on the language which applied beyond specific situations); *aesthetic* (initially this would represent substantive knowledge based on myths and rituals, but was separated from it, focusing on the creation and art); and *theoretical* (facilitated by writing, representing a form of thinking more objective and free of context and meta-knowledge, parallel to the theoretical source – it means to learn about what one knows).

But how do we appropriate – in Vygotskyan terms – knowledge accumulated by our ancestors? The ontogenetic (or individual) explanation proposed by Wells is based on a spiral that starts from experience: the meanings that we build from our participation in multiple communities of practice. From that knowledge, often informal, we come into contact with information or interpretations that have been made by the experience and meanings of others. Cognitive effort is assisted by the mediator, who gives meaning to this information based on his experience born out of the construction of knowledge, and the learner participates in social activity. Finally, we come to understanding when the construction of knowledge is reinterpreted personally – we "appropriate" it, based on personal experience and prior knowledge – and it ends up being modified or improved. Logically, the author says, the resulting experience is the new starting point for a new cycle of learning, in a spiral. We learn, deeply.

However, there is not a mediator who knows how to teach in all learning situations. In general, in informal contexts this is not so. Individuals and organizations learn things that are not stable – that have not been defined or understood previously. And they learn as the knowledge is created. In the current social context, when the pressures for change become intense and the contradictions in human activities are accelerated, a new way of learning appears. Yrjö Engeström, director of the Center for Activity Theory and Developmental Work Research of the University of Helsinki, calls it expanded learning (Engeström, 1987).

This new form of learning explains how we learn knowledge that is not yet available. For first-order (reproductive) and second-order (researcher) learning, we can use the explanatory frameworks already mentioned. But for learning of the third order, which questions the available practices, the theory of expanded knowledge comes into play (complementary to Vygotskyan ideas), suggesting that learning and development can follow a horizontal movement, rather than the vertical movement – allowing us to achieve deeper levels of knowledge rather than higher degrees of competition.

The contradiction between the accepted practices and new needs leads us to question and to seek, through horizontal movement, alternative forms of knowledge, which receive feedback from other people and are negotiated and finally agreed upon. All this leads to collective ZPDs, in which the processes of learning and teaching are bidirectional and complex (Engeström, 1999).

Learning lengthwise with height and width throughout all of our lives leads us to think that teaching and learning will be every day in the knowledge society. Learning will be as common as buying, playing, or going to the bank (Longworth, 2003). And if we have to be learning in three dimensions, it is logical to think that it is impossible to do so only through professional teachers. The other side of the coin – teaching – will have to be democratized, and we are all going to have to not only learn, but also teach – or, better still, be involved in learning by teaching.

Chapter 3

Learning by teaching

What do we know?

By contributing to the joint meaning making with and for others, one also makes meaning
for oneself and, in the process, extends one's own understanding.

Gordon Wells (1999: p108)

In this chapter, we will link some ideas contained in the preceding pages to reveal an explanatory framework which incorporates pedagogical experiences, long since developed in school contexts, in which students act as teachers of their own peers. These practices were concerned with the learning of the participants, and provided the first empirical data of what we are calling learning by teaching. In the second part of the chapter, we will review the evidence from research about the concept of learning by teaching, as well as the potential and limitations of this learning device.

Students as mediators and teachers

As discussed in the previous chapter, the Zone of Proximal Development (ZPD), a concept coming from the sociocultural theory developed from the ideas of Vygotsky, enables learning as a subjective restructuring process (internalization) from instruments of cultural mediation in terms of social interaction (intersubjectivity). The ZPD, space between what one is able to make alone in terms of actual development and what one is able to do with the help of others, defines the area where mediator supports are likely to promote learning, because it is a bit advanced on what one already knows, but not so far away as to make it incomprehensible.

The concept of ZPD has great appeal in explaining educational performance, where mediators must know the levels of development of their students (both real and potential) in order to delimit the zone where the teacher's performance is going to be fruitful, in terms of promoting learning. This applied to formal education has resulted in what Wells (1999) called "expanded interpretation", which holds the following to be true of the ZPD:

*   It emerges from the activity, and is created in the interaction between the participants. It is not an individual attribute of the apprentice. When the participants solve problems or build solutions together, they expand the potential for new learning.

- It is an opportunity to learn with others and from others, applying potentially to all participants, and not just the least expert. This idea is based, as we shall see later, on the potential of learning by offering educational assistance to others.
- It uses sources of guidance and support that are not limited to human participants physically present; they may include participants absent, but recovered through memory or books or other sources of information.
- It involves all aspects of the participant, not only their cognition. Learning involves acting, thinking and feeling. Therefore, it changes the identity of the participant and consequently transforms communities and practices.

A key element in this process of cooperation for social learning construction is the role of the mediator, understood as operating between the mental activity of the apprentice and the new information. In the school context the mediator has been identified, traditionally, with the teacher. However, in the Vygotskyan conception, the mediator may be any adult or more capable peer.

The possibility of a more competent student, in a specific skill, acting as a mediator of another fellow student results in what has been generically termed peer learning. Derived from this concept, studies cover a multitude of development contexts, such as the relationship between siblings, showing that little brothers tend to admire the older ones, who serve as models and tutors throughout childhood (Buhrmester & Furman, 1990). They also do it effectively in relation to other peers, because they are highly engaged in aid, providing detailed and stimulating instruction (Azmitia & Hesser, 1993). But perhaps more relevant here are the comparative studies between the mediating role of adults and of children.

Most of these works agree upon the superiority of the mediation of the adult to that of a child. For instance, a comparative study of pairs of children and pairs of mothers and children showed that mothers offered more effective aid within the ZPD than did children (McLane, 1987). But the best known of these studies are those of Barbara Rogoff (1990), who found that adults are better teachers than children, because they help the child to go beyond the immediate objective, provide relevant information, teach strategies for generalization, use more verbal information and know the apprentice level better. In short, the adult is more capable of assuming the dynamic role in the process of guided participation.

However, it should be noted that in these studies there is no initial training for child tutors and that the interaction between the pair is spontaneous. It depends, therefore, on the degree of ability of the tutor and their emotional involvement in the learning of their partner. In formal education contexts, these conditions can be modified (by offering tutors training, for example) or be neutralized (by the disappearance of the difference in emotional involvement between the mother and the child), to stimulate emotional relationships between fellow students.

In the context of formal education, it seems that the contextual conditions are no longer as favourable to the adult (now played by the teacher) – especially as the prototypical constraints of the traditional classroom make it very difficult (if not impossible) to establish generalized one-on-one interaction between teachers and students.

Of course there are interesting initiatives to alter this kind of organization of one teacher to many students. There are, for example, co-teaching initiatives: two teachers in the classroom (referred to in the last chapter). However, we note the harmful consequences that the directional kind of classroom organization can have – characterized by a monopoly of the ability to teach in the hands of teachers. In the first place, a low proportion of pedagogical aid reaches students when they are limited to one source of aid to learning (the teacher); it is difficult to adjust aid to the personal needs experienced by every one of our students. These elements have often resulted in a deep feeling of frustration in teachers, as they feel that they are unable to respond to the personal needs of their students.

But despite regular classrooms – with a single teacher to many students – it is possible to organize one-to-one interactions between students. And in that school context, there are studies (e.g. Good & Brophy, 1997) which show that, under certain conditions, peer mediation is more effective than adult mediation, since student tutors (1) more easily make use of vocabulary and examples appropriate to the age of their peers, (2) are recent apprentices of the material, (3) are familiar with the potential frustrations and problems of the new apprentice and (4) tend to be more direct in the resolution of doubts.

All who have teaching experience have lived the experience of a student asking for help because he or she doesn't understand something. We try to explain it, in thirty seconds … one minute … a minute and a half … and suddenly his or her partner says a couple of words and, as if by magic, our student instantly understands. Greenwood, Carta and Kamps (1990) compared the advantages and disadvantages of mediation by teachers versus mediation by peers, in the conventional classroom. They understand the mediation of the teacher is for all students in the class, while peer mediation can be done in the privileged format of one-to-one. In Table 3.1, we collect their conclusions.

Please note that the authors restrict pedagogical support to the assistance provided by the teacher. But if interactions offered by students in peer-learning formats seek to provide mutual aid to learn, it would be logical that the amount of provision of pedagogical support is higher in these formats than in the collective interaction of the teacher.

Assessing the advantages and disadvantages of the use of the mediation, it seems that it is essential that teachers learn to share the ability to mediate that they previously monopolized, in order to turn our classrooms into communities where students learn not only through educational support provided by the teacher but also through mutual support offered among the students.

The contributions of sociocultural research on peer learning (e.g. Hogan & Tudge, 1999) helped us to become aware of the factors involved in developing peer interactions in peer learning. These factors indicated whether to ensure the student mediator was a little more expert; that there was adjustment to the level of

Table 3.1 Mediation of adult versus peer mediation in school education

Advantages	Teacher	Peer
Teacher–student ratio (proportion of pedagogical assistance)	High	Low
Engaged time	Variable	High
Opportunity to respond	Low	High
Opportunity to correct errors	Low	High
Immediacy in error correction	Low	High
Opportunity to help and encourage	Low	High
Opportunity to cooperate	Low	High
Motivation	From teacher	From teacher and peer
Economic cost	High	Low
Disadvantages		
Requirement of prior training	Low	High
Quality control requirement	Low	High
Material requirements	High	Low
Clash with traditional school practice	No	Yes

reasoning, the difficulty of the task and their support to the mate, and that interaction was organized in such a way that the expert student gave the explanations.

It seems that the ZPD between peers stands out for the following inter-psychological processes (Colomina & Onrubia, 2001): conflict between moderately divergent views (cognitive conflict or conceptual disputes); mutual adjustment through language (by making explicit the student's own point of view, obtaining adjusted aid and co-construction of ideas); and support for the attribution of meaning to learning (interdependence of objectives, resources and rewards and psycho-social relations).

The distinction proposed by Damon and Phelps (1989) on the continuum of dimensions or scenarios of educational peer interactions is already classic. From the characteristics of the members, the objectives and the type of interaction, the authors distinguish among the following:

- *Tutoring:* a relationship between two students presenting different skill levels on a specific topic.

- *Cooperation:* the relationship, acquisition or application of knowledge, established among a group of students with heterogeneous skills within boundaries.
- *Collaboration:* a relationship focused on the acquisition and/or application of knowledge by two or more students with similar abilities.

With respect to the type of interaction, Damon and Phelps refer to two elements. In the first, referring to the degree of equality or symmetry of the role of the members of the interaction, relations are characterized as symmetrical, equal, or asymmetric, with regard to the different roles. In the second, the degree of mutual interaction is analysed: the connection, the depth and the bidirectionality of communicative transactions. Table 3.2 summarizes this classification of interactions based on their quality.

As shown, in peer tutoring equality is low, so that each student plays a different role, depending on whether they are a tutor or tutee. While mutuality can be variable, depending on the receptivity of the tutee, in general it will tend to be low, since it is dominated by tutor interaction.

In cooperation, roles developed by students are relatively similar, or you have a level of equivalent responsibility. Therefore, a general symmetry relationship is produced, although at certain times asymmetries are offsetting. The mutuality is medium and depends on competition among teams, the distribution of responsibilities or roles among members and the extrinsic or intrinsic reward.

In collaboration, equality among members is high, since they share a similar level of ability to problem solve. And mutuality is also high, since all subjects contribute to the interaction on an equal footing.

Although the authors conceived the three scenarios – peer tutoring, cooperation and collaboration – as a continuum of interactions, needless to say this distinction is not so clear in practice. This is not only because in cooperative learning, elements of other situations occur, but also because some of the essential characteristics of each

Table 3.2 Characteristics of the dimensions of peer learning

	Tutoring	Cooperation	Collaboration
Equality Symmetry	Low Asymmetrical	High Symmetrical	High Symmetrical
Mutuality	Low	Medium	High
Knowledge	Unidirectional Transmission (in archaic definition)	Multidirectional Transmission/transforming consensual	Bidirectional Transformation (negotiated)
ZPD	Tutees help tutoring	Fluid and dynamic	Fluid and dynamic
Speech	One way (in archaic definition)	Uni- and Multidirectional	Bidirectional

one of them can be seen to be engaged in educational practice. Thus, for example, Ellis and Gauvin (1992) question the equal or symmetrical nature of the collaboration in dyads of students with informal interactions which are not externally organized by the teacher – they can easily tend to be dominated by one of the group.

McCarthey and McMahon (1992), from a social constructivist perspective, characterized each of these three dimensions of peer learning in relation to the concept of learning, the ZPD and speech, as is synthesized in Table 3.2. For these authors, in peer tutoring knowledge goes from one individual to another in a unidirectional way, from the tutor to the tutee. This holds the idea of knowledge as transmission, in the sense that it is the tutor who structures the learning process. Tutors do this precisely acting within the ZPD, because their actual developmental level is higher, being more skilful that their tutees. Seen thus, speech is essentially unidirectional, tutor to tutee, with dialogue limited to the activity of work and the tutor's reproduction of the role of the traditional teacher.

It is worth saying (as we will see in the next chapter) that this analysis is greatly disputed by the current trends of peer tutoring, in which the definition of peer tutoring is reformulated. Keith Topping, an expert on peer tutoring, distinguished between (1) the archaic vision based on the linear model of transmission of knowledge, where the tutor was seen as a mere substitute for the teacher, that could even act with a small group of apprentices (Topping, 1996); and (2) the current conception, which defines peer tutoring in terms of individuals belonging to socially similar groups, where none is a professional teacher of the other, and they help one another to learn while learning themselves (Topping, 2005).

In cooperation, knowledge flows within the group in a multidirectional way, not necessarily just to one other student. The task makes several students transmit knowledge, and this is transformed by the interactive processes of negotiation and appropriation. The students build knowledge jointly and, depending on the task, the ablest student attends to others within the ZPD. But to permanently change this role over time, relations are fluid and dynamic, and nobody is responsible for transfer control – unlike in tutoring. Speech is only episodically unidirectional in a context of multidirectionality.

With respect to peer interactions based on collaboration, McCarthey and McMahon emphasize the joint construction of knowledge from multidirectionality and joint transformation. The implications of the ZPD are identical to those in cooperative learning situations. Speech is also bidirectional and allows a fluid dialogue, the responsibility shared with the partner or group.

In the next chapter, when we talk about reciprocal peer tutoring (Fantuzzo & Ginsburg-Block, 1998), where tutor and tutee periodically alternate their role, we will see how the division into three dimensions that has been presented here has primarily an academic nature and can serve to help understand temporarily isolated episodes of peer learning. In more protracted processes in time (when people work as a team), the dimensions that we have characterized alternate. So in the same group of students, a student who at one point acts as a tutor can work as a tutee or collaboratively on another occasion.

Both perspectives of theoretical and educational practice locate cooperation in the centre of the continuum of peer-learning scenarios. In fact, the denomination of cooperation or cooperative learning often accommodates instructional practices that involve tutoring and collaboration. No wonder, then, that the heading *cooperative learning* is recognized historically as the main contributor in these three scenarios.

Despite this, at this point there is no unique position. Some authors (O'Donnell & King, 1999; Dillenbourg, 1999) prefer to use the term "collaborative learning" as the umbrella or more general term that encompasses the different dimensions of peer learning. It is true that collaboration can be seen as a form of peer learning which is more natural and spontaneous. The others, cooperation and tutoring, require a certain degree of organization or artificiality and a certain level of structuring of interaction. Other specialists have chosen to avoid the controversial cooperation–collaboration issue, which has its origin in the Latin of the origin of both words, and use alternative terms such as *Peer Assisted Learning* (Topping & Ehly, 1998) or describe the relationships established between students in a precise way (e.g. tutoring, monitoring and peer assessment).

In our opinion, this controversy is not very productive, and as we will suggest later, all three scenarios can comply with the conditions that the literature identifies as necessary for cooperation. It will be important to recognize that structuring the interaction between members of the team – as in peer tutoring and cooperative learning – is the key to success, at least in contexts where participants have difficulties in developing complex social skills required to work with others (Topping, Buchs, Duran & Van Keer, 2017).

Of the three stages of the continuum of peer learning, in only one of these are students explicitly entrusted with the development of the role of "teacher": peer tutoring. It seems logical that first evidence dealing with the learning of whoever teaches should come precisely from such school practices. Given that tutors are students, in a status of apprentice within the institution, they might find it desirable to tutor a fellow student and also find this had some effect on their own learning. Peer tutoring allows students not only to be substitute teachers, but also to learn themselves – which is of course considered typical of the student.

Evidence of tutor learning

By the end of the 1960s, studies documenting students who had been helping their struggling peers to improve their reading found the tutors progressed more in reading than did their peer tutees (Cloward, 1967). This evidence of the peer tutors' learning, in their role as teacher, is also found in the results of the first reviews or meta-analyses on the subject. The first one, Allen (1976), ratifies the learning of tutors in the diversity of studies on educational experiences analysed. A meta-analysis conducted by Cohen, Kulik and Kulik (1982) confirms the positive effects (academic and attitudes) for tutors. An interesting review by Goodlad and Hirst (1989) compiles research that supports cognitive gains for tutors, to the point that their book is titled *Peer Tutoring: A guide to learning by teaching.*

Positive outcomes of student learning by tutors claimed attention and interest in the explanation of the phenomenon of learning by teaching. Everything seemed to indicate that teaching produces a richer experience than learning for oneself, because it helps people to specify their own ideas and supports a context to construct different knowledge from that they would use when learning alone (Kafai & Harel, 1991).

But what really explains this learning potential that seems akin to the activity of teaching? At what point does it occur? When preparing classes? When giving them? To try to report the available evidence and integrate it into an explanatory framework, we will consider the different elements that occur in the complex process of teaching: preparation (pre-active behaviours of the teacher or the peer tutor), explanation and feedback (interactive behaviours) and reflection (post-active behaviours).

Learning to teach: better than learning for oneself

It seems that learning something for yourself or learning to teach others arouses different mental processes. In 1971, Alan Gartner and Frank Riessmann, who later founded the Peer Research Laboratory at the University of New York, synthesized the cognitive benefits that seem to take place in the course of preparing to teach (Gartner, Kohler & Riessmann, 1971). At this stage, prior to the encounter with the apprentice, the teacher or the tutor must do the following:

- Review the material. Even when this is known, the review can help to deepen understanding of the subject in a more complex way.
- Organize the material for its presentation. This process can lead teachers to find new examples and illustrations that help explain the material. In addition, teachers must reorganize information in a new way, reformulating their own knowledge.
- Identify the basic structure – the fundamental or essential points – with primary items in front of those which are secondary, something that allows teachers to understand the material more deeply.

Ernest Rutherford (1871–1937), who won the Nobel Prize in chemistry in 1908, believed that a scientific discovery was not completed until it was explained to others (Highet, 1950). In the same vein, there is a quote attributed to Einstein that reads: "If you can't explain it simply, then you don't understand it well enough".

These general ideas, which all those who have teaching experience can recognize, were contrasted in the classic work of Bargh and Schul (1980), which presents the results of an experiment where students who learn for themselves (to pass a test) are compared with students who learn believing that they will teach, but in reality do not. This last effect is called *expectancy*: learning *to* teach (but not really teaching). The results were favourable to students who learned hoping to teach what they studied; and the authors confirmed that this condition (learning to teach) altered the process of learning, promoting a greater effort in selecting the relevant elements and organizing them into a representation.

This initial work, however, had significant limitations (especially those derived from an experiment outside of the school context). But it aroused interest and encouraged further work, as in the replication of Benware and Deci (1984), who got results in a school that also suggested that preparing for teaching helped students to make greater efforts to better organize the information. In addition, *expectancy* improves the teachers' (or student who learns to teach) motivation, because they try to avoid embarrassment (that teachers often feel) from not knowing the answer.

Recent studies show that expectancy may enhance the learning of declarative knowledge, like academic content (Fiorella & Mayer, 2013; Nestojko et al., 2014) as well as motor learning (Daou, Lohse & Miller, 2016).

To learn and explain: better than just learning to teach

Subsequent studies added the possibility that participants had to explain what they had learned. This research is very relevant because it will help us to understand if teachers' presentations have the potential for learning for themselves and provide evidence for educational practices that we will present in the next chapter, based on learning through elaborating materials or explanations for potential apprentices.

Explaining to others is a way to test the review and reformulation of the information that our mind has gathered to transform it into knowledge. Just as children explain the lesson to their parents (in the process of learning and before facing the teacher), we explain our ideas to our partners, friends or colleagues, and often experience the feeling of finishing off, ordering and securing our thinking by this means. That tends to be so, even if the others have not opened their mouths. It is what is known as audience effect (Zajonc, 1966).

The outstanding work here is from Linda Annis (1983). Her research, with an impeccable experimental design, distributed 130 students over five different situations, with regard to the learning of content. To some, the content was taught; others read it; others read it and it was taught; others learned to teach it, but were not allowed to actually teach it (*expectancy*); and, finally, others learned it and explained it through teaching. Controlling the intervening variables (e.g. equivalence of groups, activities), students were assessed with respect to their understanding of content and cognitive benefits. Students who were teachers were better, but especially those who had the opportunity to actually effectively teach.

Annis agreed with previous works that teaching others favoured verbal learning and required more attention to what you have to teach (and learn). It required having it personally coded (appropriate content rebuilt in the mind). It also required associating it with prior knowledge. Such cognitive benefits were not only a product of preparing to teach, but also of actually presenting the material to the tutee. Although Annis points out that interaction is also responsible for tutor learning, her work focused on the expository explanation. Future research, presented in the next section ("Teaching interaction"), allows interactive explanation to be taken into account.

Following this work, other researchers provided similar results in favour of higher learning outcomes for students who learn and explain, as compared with those who are limited to learn in order to teach (e.g. Ehly, Keith & Bratton, 1987), even controlling for the variable content – making the students themselves work on various topics (Lambiotte, Dansereau, O'Donnell, Young, Skaggs & Hall, 1987).

In fact, the comparison between these two situations of learning by teaching (*learning to teach* and *learning by explaining*) continues to this day. A more recent study (Fiorella & Mayer, 2013) argues that both promote learning, but the opportunity to explain what the tutors learned is superior when evaluation takes the subject on a long-term basis, indicating that explaining to others enables deeper and higher quality learning. The authors interpret a finding from the theory of multimedia learning (Mayer & Wittrock, 2006), which holds that teaching facilitates the selection of the most relevant information, its organization into representations which make sense and its integration into prior knowledge.

All this would seem to lead us to see explanation as the responsible element in learning by teaching. But things, as always, are somewhat more complex. Research argues that self-explanation – which in fact is what we do when we learn for ourselves, but also when we learn to teach – promotes cognitive activities that lead to acquiring new knowledge (Chi, Bassok, Lewis, Reimann & Glaser, 1989). During the construction of self-explanations, we learn through the identification of knowledge what we are missing and are able to acquire through inductive or deductive processes. In principle, these same mechanisms responsible for learning in the construction of self-explanations should be relevant in explanations to others.

And not only that, Webb (1989) argues that to explain to another potentially offers more opportunities to learn than to explain to yourself. We will not only learn by identifying what we don't know, but also because the person receiving the explanation identifies gaps and inconsistencies, and demands clarifications or confrontations from different or alternative points of view. To resolve these discrepancies, the explainer has to search for new information and build deeper knowledge. We note here that Webb sees the tutor in an interactive process with the apprentice, when until now we have focused only on presenting in front of an anonymous or passive listener.

But this supremacy of the explanation to others against the explanation to oneself is not always supported by the research. Ploetzner, Dillenbourg, Praier and Traum (1999) distinguished five levels of interactivity in explanations: explain to yourself, explain to an anonymous listener, explain to a passive listener, explain to someone with limited response and explain mutually. And these authors reported some works that did not find substantial differences between self-explanation and explaining to others, although they did themselves identify some problems of procedure in such research: for example, that the self-explanations could be aimed not only to oneself, but also to the expert; or that the status of the expert could make students better prepare their self-explanations than explanations to their peers.

A very thorough review of research on the tutor's learning in peer tutoring practices by Rod Roscoe and Michelene Chi (2007) from the University of Arizona offers light on this controversy. The point of departure for these authors is that, as in self-explanation, the explanation to others offers rich opportunities for the tutor (the student in the role of teacher), who is involved in the process of *reflective knowledge building* that leads to learning. Tutors have to produce explanations of quality, recognize their own points of improvement, use them to reorganize their own knowledge and generate inferences to repair the errors. In addition, the use of examples or different representations, common in the explanations, may allow them to deepen their knowledge.

For all these reasons, tutors should engage in an important metacognitive activity: they should evaluate their own knowledge and understanding and see if their explanations make sense and are logical. However, other research indicates that tutors do not always take advantage of the opportunity afforded them in their role of learning by explaining. It seems that rather than *building* knowledge, many tutors are limited to *saying* knowledge (*knowledge telling*). They tend to offer explanations of response built on questions, and summarize information or describe procedures with little preparation or construction. The review authors conclude that *saying* knowledge can impact positively on the tutor's own learning (securing memory) and is at the base of the construction process. But it is a pity that tutors do not always use their role to go a little further, to learn more and better, through building knowledge.

Further work from one of those authors (Roscoe, 2014) argues that tutors would also have their own ZPD, including between what they are able to teach and reason but have not yet had the opportunity to teach. It seems key to teach student tutors how to explore the emergence of challenges and how to synthesize basic concepts and information.

Some of the research that our teams have developed involved Catalan pupils who acted as tutors of Spanish for Scottish pupils, who in turn acted as English tutors for the Catalan pupils (Thurston, Duran, Cunningham, Blanch & Topping, 2009). In pairs, they had to provide feedback for the improvement of the texts produced by each student in the second language. In a first phase of the research, students in their role as tutor decided the level of support for the errors that their tutee produced. The tendency was to *say* knowledge, offering built or correct responses (e.g. writing the phrase well), instead of offering clues, so tutoring by itself helped the tutee repair the mistake. This they did in a second phase of this research, when they received initial training to do so (Topping, Dehkinet, Blanch, Corcelles & Duran, 2013).

As a result, not all forms of explaining have the same implications for learning for those who teach. This tendency of tutors to *say* knowledge has a strong relationship with the transmissive teaching and learning concept which is the basis of traditional instructional practices, which we have seen in the previous chapter. It also explains why some teachers tell us they have the impression that they learned through teaching the first time they prepared material, but then when they teach it again and again they fail to learn it better, and rather they unlearn it. Perhaps these teachers learned in the proactive phase (learned to teach it), but not during the explanation, since they limited the way they explained the information to their students.

There is another group of research that is worth considering here. Rather than give an account of the reasons why learning occurs by teaching, this research uses this potential for the development of instructional models supported by information and communication technologies: what these authors call the *learning by teaching paradigm*. In this sense, Biswas, Schwartz, Leelawong and Vye (2005) have designed *teachable agents* (computer programs that simulate an apprentice who should be taught), so that the student in the role of tutor can learn by teaching. So, for example, high school students learn the ecosystem of rivers by teaching it to Betty's Brain. The process requires explaining to Betty through a conceptual map, asking causal questions and putting Betty to the test. It goes without saying that the purpose is not to have the machine learn, but to have the student learn.

This research line is rich and suggestive, since it poses varying degrees of interaction with the *learning-by-teaching agents* (Leelalawong, 2005). In this way, they create situations like the following:

- Agents that learn directly from the information provided by the users (i.e. here students that learning by teaching), through, for example, conceptual maps. At the same time, some agents allow the user to see their representations (the causal maps that are being developed, following the example), while others do not.
- Agents that learn indirectly, or use representations of the information different from the one the users employed to prepare the explanation.

The software simulating the mind of the learner is quick and allows the group to obtain interesting results. This work has been extended to primary education (Chase, Chin, Oppezzo & Schwartz, 2009) and even to early childhood (Anderberg, Axelsson, Bengtsson, Hakansson & Lindberg, 2013). In addition, the research is incorporating progressively higher degrees of interaction and agents are becoming near in appearance to human, as with the SimStudents (Matsuda, Yarzebinski, Keiser, Raizada, Cohen, Stylianides & Koedinger, 2013).

Surely, some of us could have doubts about whether it is worthwhile to devote so much effort to place the tutor in front of an artificial intelligence, which can hardly offer the richness and complexity of the mind of the human partner. But we must pay close attention to these works, because they control a variable of utmost importance in research on peer learning: the other. We all know that depending on how you perceive the other person, you can generate more or less help for teaching him or her. And of course, these works are providing clear evidence about learning by teaching, and specifically about learning by explaining in the construction of knowledge.

Teaching interacting: better than teaching and explaining

We have seen how research shows that the role of educator (teacher or peer tutor) potentially offers learning opportunities for those involved: we learn to teach and we learn by explaining, especially when we build knowledge. So far, the apprentice has played a passive or limited role. But what happens in the learning experience of educators if they interact with their learners? What effects can dialogue with students have on the learning of the tutee and of the tutor? Questioning (asking questions to the students and answering their questions), observation and experimentation – what effects will these have on the learning of the educator?

Again, the work of Roscoe and Chi (2007), reviewing research in peer tutoring, offers us light on the question. Questioning – that includes both asking and responding to questions – is the other activity, together with the explanation. The tutors introduce issues and guide and follow the thinking of their tutees. At the same time, they have to answer information or clarification requirements arising from the confusion of the tutee. So, asking and responding to questions that arise should support the learning of the tutors.

Unlike questions from tutors, tutee questions have received much attention in the research. Asking means putting a problem into words: articulating the question to provoke a response. This may involve organizing and integrating concepts and high-level reasoning. But, sometimes, students are looking for a simple confirmation of what they think is right. The question becomes more beneficial when questions are deeper, and when they require integration of prior and new knowledge, reorganization of mental models, inferences and metacognitive self-regulation (King, 1998).

Tutors can benefit from the construction of questions that help the tutee to think in depth about the material. They can ask about contrasting concepts, apply them and find causal relationships. Therefore, tutors have to think to generate issues, but also consider the fundamental ideas, relationships and principles needed to produce a correct answer. In this way, they reorganize and reinforce their own understanding, and they have the opportunity to discover their own gaps or misunderstandings. So, to question (ask and answer questions of tutees) can promote the involvement of tutors in the reflective construction of their own knowledge and learning. Their replies to deep questions can help the tutor to overcome only *saying* the knowledge.

Research by Roscoe and Chi shows that spontaneously tutors tend to *say* knowledge, except when having received training to go beyond this, like Catalan and Scottish students did. In measures of comprehension and recall, trained tutors ask and respond with integration, application and reasoning, outperforming less trained tutors. At the same time, studies that have focused on the analysis of the interaction between tutor and tutee (not only on final results) show evidence of the benefits of answering questions by the tutor. The tutee questions start a collaborative dialogue enhancing joint understanding. The quality of the questions is a key factor in explaining reflective construction of knowledge. But, unfortunately, we do not have studies dedicated to specifically analysing the benefits to the tutors of their own questions. If questioning, especially when it moves from *saying* knowledge, has strong potential to support the tutor's learning, we must ask ourselves whether common teaching and learning contexts allow or encourage this form of interaction.

It is well known that the classical structure of educational discourse in the classroom is the so-called structure IRF (Sinclair & Coulthard, 1975), holding that the sequence of interaction between teacher and students consists of three phases: an initiation (I), which is normally generated by the teacher and often takes the form of question; the second, a student response (R); and third, the teacher's feedback (F) to the pupil's response.

Some authors have considered that this pattern describes speech too directed and controlled by the teacher who, in addition, tends to make questions with known answers. Wells (1999), for example, proposes a reinterpretation of the third component, the *feedback* (F), which exceeds a limited evaluation perspective and involves tracking and the possibility of new cycles of exchanges through language. Perhaps this limited pattern well explains the exchange of interactions between a teacher and a lot of students that often characterizes conventional classes. But what happens in one-to-one contexts, as in peer tutoring?

If the IRF pattern is such that usually students are in common learning situations with their teachers, pairs of students tend to follow it in spontaneous tutoring (Graesser, D'Mello & Cade, 2009). But in the case of tutoring where students receive initial training to confront the resolution of doubts and problems together, there is a change in the structure of the pattern of interaction, going from three phases to five. This richer structure, that Graesser and Person (1994) called IRFCE, is that the tutor poses a problem (*initial*); tutees provide an initial response (*response*); the tutor offers a small amount of feedback, depending on the quality of the response (*feedback*); tutor and tutee establish a round of dialogue to improve the quality of the first reply (*collaboration*); and, finally, the tutor evaluates if the tutee well understands the response (*evaluation*).

In the interaction between students, IRF's tripartite structure is enriched, and the most interesting processes happen in the phase of collaboration, where participants develop a joint action to build knowledge (Graesser, Bowers, Hacker & Person, 1997), rather than just speaking it. At this stage, the tutors, recognizing the ZPD, offer adjusted aid with different levels of scaffolding through different types of dialogic behaviours:

- *Hinting:* Insinuate, give clues, avoid the direct response, allow sharing the responsibility for the resolution of the activity or the cognitive load.
- *Prompting*: Inducement to have the tutee complete knowledge with relevant information.
- *Splicing*: Joining, adjusting, or binding. The conversation is interwoven as it unfolds and takes on significance. This requires a high degree of cooperation. The tutors are careful to enter correct information and correct or complete answers.
- *Pumping*: Extract information. The tutor gets information from the tutee through positive or neutral feedback, or with explicit demands. The tutor can put more cognitive load on the tutee and check if he or she reasons correctly or makes errors in understanding.
- *Summarizing:* After the joint construction of the correct answer or solution to the problem, the tutor can ask the tutee do it alone and thus be able to demonstrate mastery of the content.

In the same vein, to identify patterns of interaction in peer tutoring contexts, Duran & Monereo (2005) researched fixed and reciprocal peer tutoring in writing, which indicated the presence of three types of interaction:

- IRF, or traditional sequence. The prototype sequence is present, but in the third step feedback (F) generates new messages, giving feedback to the tutee and generating a new cycle of discursive interaction.
- IRCE, or tutorial sequence. The first two acts (I, R) match the previous sequence, but then a sequence of cooperation, guided by the tutor, is produced, which is

improved through a cycle of cooperative exchanges (C) – splicing and hinting – ending with a response that finally the tutor evaluates (E). It is a typical sequence of fixed tutoring dominated by the tutor.

- ICE, or collaborative sequence. Starting with the initiation (I), but from here the two members of the pair (tutor and tutee) enter into a cycle of cooperation (C) to jointly build the response – through questioning and splicing. After this constructive response cycle, evaluation (E) by the tutor occurs. It is a sequence of reciprocal tutoring.

All these processes occur in the rich interaction that allows peer learning to bring us closer to the building of knowledge by the tutor in the context of the interaction with his or her tutee. The increased opportunities for interaction between the teacher and the learner can be responsible for learning, not only for the apprentice, but also for the educator.

From a very different perspective, but with results completely aligned with those presented so far, we would like to make reference to interesting research carried out by Claudio Cortese from the University of Turin. In order to explore the ways in which learning takes place in different organizations (e.g. industrial, services, administration or public health), Cortese (2005) proposed collecting evidence from personal learning experiences, through 282 interviews of great depth (8 to 10 hours) with professionals of different areas and employment levels, none of them linked to professional teaching. With an interview technique eliciting previous knowledge, informants told of the moments in their working lives when they had learned the most. Most learning experiences were in this order: participating in reflection or discussion groups; reading; receiving training from a superior; receiving help or advice of colleagues; through the experience of others, in training classes; through their own experience; and teaching others.

Analysing these episodes of learning through teaching, the author identifies three types of processes taking place:

- Observing. Teaching allows watching the apprentice and seeing him developing the task (directly, when modelling; or indirectly, thorough the performance of the apprentice). It is not only observing the tutee, but the impact of what we have taught him. Okita and Schwartz (2013) suggest that observing the tutee receiving feedback has more potential for learning than does directly receiving feedback. Observation allows the tutor to recover knowledge (sometimes forgotten) and reorganize it, becoming aware of it, going from tacit or implicit knowledge to an explicit knowledge that can be codified, communicated and transferred; that is, that will spring from the individual to be an "organizational" knowledge (Eraut, 2000).
- Listening. Teaching allows listening to the apprentice and becoming aware of procedures, often hidden by routine, especially when the apprentice poses problems, doubts or fears about competence or professional values. This process can trigger episodes of cooperative learning.

- Experiencing. Teaching often allows testing alternative work methods and innovation processes, from issues or points of view suggested by the apprentice or emerging from joint work.

For Cortese, the role of teacher (tutor, instructor, coach, mentor, expert) in professional fields has a high potential for learning. And this is because teaching involves four elements:

1 Encountering diversity. Teaching requires recognizing the diversity of each other, appreciating it and therefore being decentralized from self and observing oneself through the eyes of others.
2 Individual reflection. Teaching offers the possibility of spending time progressively "doing", "thinking" and finally "communicating", which promotes learning. Teaching allows exposure to unforeseen problems, often pointed out by the apprentice or arising from unexpected situations, and these problems often are not in the manuals. Teaching promotes dialogue, which by its very nature is social and essential for learning. It takes place in a context where the power relations are such that the tutor is in control while allowing the tutee to ask questions, creating cognitive conflicts and providing pedagogical support or assessment.
3 Public reflection. If individual reflection has a high potential for learning, reflection in public, in the presence of others, has even more, because this allows us to recognize our own emotions in others and engage in a process of mutual support, ultimately allowing change.
4 Meta-ignorance. Teaching allows awareness of our own gaps or "empty spaces" in our personal representation of the reality of the issues unanswered, questions that need answering, and that we need to ask ourselves – the knowledge that we must review, however erroneous, inaccurate or obsolete. The consciousness of ignorance is a prerequisite for learning.

Cortese (2005) concludes that it is necessary that the interaction between teacher and learner is bidirectional, encouraging learners to interact with each other, asking questions, proposing topics and creating challenges for the tutor. Teaching offers little chance of learning when it is done in a unidirectional way – from teacher to student – as in the memoristic or transmissive conception of teaching and learning.

Everything suggests that we have scientific evidence and sufficient knowledge to understand the potential of learning by teaching. We learn to teach (in the proactive phase); we learn by explaining and interacting with learners through questioning, collaboration and observation (in the interactive phase). We learn – as we will see in the last chapter – reflecting on what we taught and how we have taught it (in the post-active phase).

If we learn throughout the process of teaching, why do we not give our students more opportunities to learn by teaching others? In the next chapter we will present social practices of learning by teaching.

Chapter 4

Learning by teaching others informally

For many years now I have been teaching Taekwondo as well as studying it. I have found that one of the best ways to learn Taekwondo is by teaching it. And many of my most important "learnings" have come by teaching kids.
Ørjan Nilsen, Instructor of Taekwondo (http://jungdokwan-taekwondo.blogspot.com.es/ 2011/10/learning-by-teaching.html)

In the second chapter we saw how informal learning that takes place in situations without educational intentionality (through activities of daily living, work, family and leisure) allows us to build knowledge and implicit theories which, although unconscious, guide our behaviour. Most of our knowledge comes from that informal learning, not only because it is the learning that occurs in our lives, outside of educational institutions, but also because the characteristics of informal learning – autonomous and voluntary, within moments of freedom, real experience and everyday life (Acaso, 2013) – generate high motivation in the apprentice and, as a result, make it extremely effective. We concluded that formal learning (which takes place in schools, colleges and universities) not only must take into account what students learn "outside" (as previous knowledge for their new learning), but also should informalize its practices to incorporate this outside knowledge into more effective ways of learning.

In this chapter, focused on informal learning, we will provide examples of opportunities to learn by teaching others, both face to face and, above all, in a virtual way, through the technologies of information and knowledge that contemporary society offers. Finally, we draw some conclusions for formal education.

Learning by teaching informally, but in person

In Chapter 1, we reflected on personal experiences of learning by teaching in everyday life and collected quotations attributed to famous teachers who have witnessed this experience, as has the instructor of Taekwondo who is quoted above. Undoubtedly this is the section where all of us can call on experiences from when we were kids and explained our lessons to our parents or our ideas to others to secure this knowledge in our minds. We will then discuss how the world of work is adopting practices of learning by teaching.

The use of a certain degree of skill or competence, achieved through personal experience or participation in communities of practice, has often been used as a platform to continue learning through providing support to less skilled persons or those with less experience. This is linked to forms of mutual aid and experiences of volunteering in the community, and we can find many interesting practices. Let's take a look at three of them, just by way of example.

Expert patient programme

Started in 2006 (Gonzàlez, Fabrellas, Agramunt, Rodríguez & Grifell, 2008) as a multidisciplinary initiative based on collaboration between patients and health professionals, the programme is based on the expert patient (EP), who uses his knowledge of the experience of chronic disease and offers this to others who suffer from the same health problem. The objectives of the programme, promoted by the Health Institute of the Catalan government, are to achieve involvement and satisfaction of patients: improve the quality of life, knowledge, habits and lifestyles; promote self-care; improve treatment adherence; reduce visits to the doctor and nurse; and decrease hospital admissions as well as visits to the emergency room.

An EP is intended to move from being a passive patient to being one who is active, informed, autonomous and committed. The proposal is clearly embodied in the framework of learning by teaching, because, above all, changes happen in the expert patient. The EPs are selected from among the group of patients who suffer chronic disease covered by the programme and meet the criteria of willingness, ability to self-care and absence of mental disabilities, as determined by an interview in which their capacities of empathy, interest in helping, motivation and communication skills are evaluated. Once selected, EPs receive training on theoretical and methodological content to be able to steer the nine sessions of 1½ hours with a dozen patients. In these sessions, health professionals develop the role of observers, intervening only if necessary and providing support and feedback to the EP.

The evaluation of the programme is carried out from surveys of knowledge, habits and lifestyles; self-management and quality of life; and the use of services with respect to visits to primary care as well as emergency and hospital admissions by comparing one year prior to intervention with a year after intervention. Following the participation of more than 2094 people (165 EPs, 484 professional observers and so on), findings are highly satisfactory, and the project allows the advance of the progressive transition from health education in a one-way mode, which is biological and dependent on the health-care professional, to another with a more experiential and social discourse (González, 2013).

Volunteering for language

In the context of restoring the Catalan language as a language of normal use after a long period of prohibition, *Voluntariat per la Llengua* (volunteers for the language) is a programme to help learning of the Catalan language through conversation. It is based on the creation of language pairs formed by a person who is fluent in Catalan and another who has basic knowledge of this language and wants to improve oral competence. It is driven by the linguistic policy of the Catalan government (www.vxl.cat).

The main objective of *Voluntariat per la Llengua* is to promote the use of Catalan in personal relationships, facilitating a communication space in which the person who has basic knowledge of Catalan and wants to acquire fluency and incorporate it in a natural way in work, daily activities or social relationships can practise with someone who speaks it fluently. To this end, the two volunteers are put in contact (the person who is a regular speaker of Catalan and the one who wants to become secure in speaking it), so they are in a real context and in a relaxed atmosphere and they speak in Catalan. It takes place for a minimum of ten hours (one hour per week for 10 weeks). Those involved only have to be of legal age and have the required language skills.

Although both persons are voluntary, the programme uses the term "volunteer" for the person who is fluent, and the person who wants to learn Catalan is known as the "apprentice". People who participate in the programme are clear that the benefit is mutual. The trainee not only improves his oral Catalan competence, but also knows society better from the activities carried out with his partner's knowledge of the environment and participation in activities organized by institutions who run the programme (lectures, conferences, cultural visits, excursions, theatre performances, etc.). The volunteer is enriched not only by the fact of knowing the culture of the other person, but also because he is forced to think about the knowledge he has of his own language, which helps to deepen and improve it in many aspects. It is an informal opportunity for learning by teaching.

Pairs are created depending on personal availability and possible common interests. The volunteer receives a brief initial training, and both members of the pair receive a brochure with basic tips for how best to work together. Support materials have been created to enrich the dialogue in meetings. For example, *Contes per parlar* (Stories to talk about), the collection *Parlem your i jo* (Let's talk about you and me) or *Llegim per parlar, llegim per aprendre* (We read to talk, we read to learn) are more focused on learning the language from reading.

The programme started in 2003, and more than 200,000 people have taken part in it. Adaptations have developed in other Catalan-speaking areas (Perpignan, Andorra, Valencia and the Balearic Islands) and in other languages in Bolzano (Italy) (www. provinz.bz.it/italian-culture/languages/1794.asp) and Flanders (Belgium) (http:// youtube.com/watch?v=BUibsiZmwGo). On September 26, 2005, the European Commission recognized it as one of the 50 best practices of learning languages which were being conducted in the European Union.

Volunteers of the Foundation Secretariado Gitano

The Fundación Secretariado Gitano (FSG) is an intercultural nonprofit organization that provides services for the development of the Roma community in Spain and in Europe. Through various programmes, the FSG provides volunteers to help the youth of this community – many of them in situations of social vulnerability – to finish compulsory education. Volunteers are students, teachers or members of the Roma community. Through extracurricular support which is provided to children and young people (in literacy, health, culture and sport), the volunteers report learning themselves in personal growth, respect, commitment to others, removal of prejudices, cooperation and the possibility of change. Even in the case of volunteers of the Roma community with no previous education, they learn what they teach and overcome personal situations of social exclusion (www.eapn.es/videos.php?v=87).

Learning by teaching at work

If these three initiatives are a small sample of the many practices based on the mobilization of social volunteering, we can also find practices that can be framed by learning by teaching in the workplace. In a society characterized by change, business organizations are increasingly based on peer learning networks or communities of practice (Blunt, 2003). Teamwork within and outside the organization is essential. The organizations which are able to respond to change show rates of learning equal to or higher than the rates of change they are facing (Guilmette, 2007). These companies are seen as learning organizations (Mayo & Lank, 2003).

In these contexts, the traditional learning of workers, based on individual development of professional careers, is moving towards collective learning, characterized by the following:

- Taking advantage of the knowledge and skills of workers (providing databases on the skills of workers that allow the assembly of short-term teams to respond to demands).
- Instant information (operating quickly via systems of transmission of messages) and instant learning (through digital and interactive resources).
- Taking advantage of incidental learning, generating registers of learning in meetings or events, and stimulating participation in social activities that are recognized and discussed, from learning opportunities both in the work process and outside of it.
- Promoting self-managed learning (with highly motivated individuals) by having group meetings where shared learning or individual knowledge is turned into organizational knowledge.

Within these contexts of learning organizations, the use of the knowledge or skill of more skilled workers becomes essential to make human capital more profitable. And this is not just true of the more skilled workers. Proposals for mentoring in the workplace – or *coaching* (Dilts, 2003) – also discover clear benefits for the mentor (Soler, 2003). Among others, these include developing intuition, patience, tolerance and social skills of supervision; receiving feedback on the courses (and learning how to receive this); adopting new and fresh ideas of tutoring (the opportunity to learn about what is taught); and increasing reputation and the valuation of what is responsible for development and institutional recognition.

The use of "intern resources" in the training plans of companies – the activity of teaching other workers through teamwork, on the Internet or through mentoring practices – offers the opportunity to turn implicit or tacit knowledge into explicit knowledge. Explicitness is important, because otherwise, if we do not use the knowledge we forget it, or it may become inaccessible to consciousness by becoming automatic (Nonaka & Takeuchi, 1995). Explicit knowledge – concerning tacit understanding, action routines or rules (Eraut, 2000) – is essential for organizational learning, since it can be coded, communicated and transferred, becoming independent of the individual and becoming part of the company culture (Cortese, 2005).

An example of a company subjected to permanent changes in its products and high staff growth that uses mentoring as a source of learning for all, including the mentor, is Intel (www.fastcompany.com/44814/inside-intels-mentoring-movement). The programme of traditional mentoring which they had was useful as a tool for the professional development of employees who wanted to move up in the company, but did not show sufficient advantage as a way of using and improving knowledge which was distributed among the professionals who worked in the company. That is why, from the New Mexico plant, they led a reformulation of mentoring that used organizational knowledge – distributed among employees – to ensure that best practices were known by workers who were being inducted.

Within this purpose there was a database, within which workers (from plant employees to senior engineers) could answer a questionnaire about their skills and knowledge. After deciding on the suitability of proposed mentors, plant workers could immediately choose a mentor who met their need for training. This feature of demanding and receiving immediate support is closely linked to the need for training to be responsive to real needs and real, practical problems. Instantly, both partners receive an email and instructions as a guide:

- The mentee, not the mentor, controls the relationship, deciding what he/she needs to learn and how. Leaving the control of the relationship (content and methodology) in the hands of the mentee not only has an impact on the motivation of the mentee and the effectiveness of pedagogical support received, but also, above all, it will generate challenges in the mentor that will become his or her own learning experiences. The company suggests a relationship should last between six and nine months.
- Specific relationships in a mentoring agreement, specifying the need for involvement of both.
- Once entered into the space, mentor and mentee decide what they do with it, while creating private-space learning which is tailored to their real needs.

In this project, mentoring is offering a new way to solve real problems, quickly and using authentic examples from the job. Beyond the benefits for the mentees, for the mentors it offers the opportunity to reflect on what they do, receive deep feedback and learn new ways to solve problems – good ways to learn when you teach.

Learning by teaching informally, through the Internet

So far we have been collecting practices and opportunities of learning involving teaching others in face-to-face situations. But what happens on the Internet? The emergence of technologies of information and knowledge has supplemented – and in some cases replaced – the informal learning that until now we had been developing in spaces such as the home, the street, the bar, or centres for socializing and leisure. Contemporary social media – through the Internet – have opened up new forms of social participation.

Information and knowledge is spread over the Internet, turning it into a distributed group intelligence located in an infinite number of nodes that are able to cooperate to deal with the challenges of knowledge, generating collective responses. The possibility of connection, and above all the possibility of participation (by selecting, mixing and re-creating or creating new knowledge), give rise to the new abundant conversation, as a process of horizontal construction of knowledge (Reig, 2012).

Participation becomes essential in this context. Thanks to blogs, wikis and collaborative platforms, the Internet has allowed millions of users to transform the role of mere consumers into that of "prosumers" (a term used extensively in Argentina's economic crisis, where in exchange networks, people acted as producers and consumers at the same time), or producers and distributors of information.

The Peer-to-Peer (P2P) phenomenon seems to be the result of the human tendency to collaborate, offering mutual support that is augmented by current technological tools. It is not a matter of sharing cultural property (music, movies, books, etc.), since multiple forms of P2P also include knowledge and personal resources of all kinds. The film *Us Now*, directed by Ivo Gormley (Banyak Films), offers many of these examples (http://banyak.co.uk/us-now/).

Among the most common Google searches (www.google.com/trends/topcharts) appear the questions that begin with "how", which lead to tutorials made by people to teach skills that respond to these questions: people who share information through forms of citizen journalism or specialized forums; people who offer personal loans for social projects or business (*crowdfunding*); those who share cars and accommodation for tourism; forms of *crowdsourcing* that cooperate to create free software (such as Linux or Firefox) in competition with giant companies; complete and multilingual encyclopaedias (Wikipedia), and so on.

Consider a network that provides members with immediate practical help on locations. I offer help about my neighbourhood, which I know well (addresses, restaurants, hotels, parties, etc.), and in exchange I can seek help from residents of other towns, if I need it. In the network (as Clay Shirky of New York University concludes in *Us Now)*, everyone is valued. In the example above, all have hands-on knowledge of our locality that could be very useful to a clueless outsider. In addition, the price of providing aid is much smaller than what you can get: you will teach less than you will learn.

But before these enormous possibilities, what do we really do? To answer this question, we should ask young people, because surely forms of their practices will extend soon to the whole population. *Digital Youth Research* (Ito et al., 2008) is an ethnographic study of three years' duration, funded by the John D. and Catherine T. MacArthur Foundation, developed by researchers at California universities to explore how young people use digital media, especially in the United States. According to its principal investigator, Mizuko Ito, this study is unique in its breadth, comprising 23 case studies, with more than 800 interviews and 5000 hours of watching online (Ito, 2012). The results explain why the intensive use of digital technologies is so absorbent and important to young people, although it worries many adults. The digital world creates new opportunities to deal with social norms, explore interests, develop technical skills and experience new forms of self-expression. The majority of young people use the Internet, driven by friendship, with the main objective being to maintain a permanent link with people in their social environment – with those who already have face-to-face contact. Social networks (like MySpace or Facebook) serve as a distraction and require the negotiation of issues of status or membership with colleagues in the local environment. In these spaces, using communication tools like Twitter or Wassap for young people, adults are not welcome.

But a smaller number of young people use the Internet, moved by their own interests, to delve beyond the information accessed through the school or local community. You can start with a Google search or by referring to chat rooms to learn more about young people's growing interests. Through trial and error, youth add new skills with the media to their repertoire, as, for example, creating a video or customizing games or personal pages. Teens share their creations and receive responses from others who are connected. With its immediacy and breadth of information, the digital world reduces the barriers that used to accompany autonomous learning, and this becomes clear in the context of peer learning.

This type of participation, encouraged by people's own interests, offers opportunities to learn through the exchange of information and support received through peer feedback. But many young people go even further, obsessed and plunging fully into any theme or specific skill. They are known as *geeks*, people with very advanced knowledge in the use and development of digital technology. But geek activity does not entail social isolation, as we might think. On the contrary, it gives rise to socialization and commitment, within specialized groups, in which can be grouped both young people and adults, all over the world. In these communities of practice, prestige and authority are accomplished through the knowledge provided. These practices, based on the autonomous construction of knowledge, peer feedback, and the recognition of providing feedback valued for others, constitute a clear framework of learning by teaching.

Let's look at some situations that can give us enlightenment, where many young people do the following:

- Create online learning resources – and learn to do this – anticipating the demands of others, at the risk of these resources not ever being used, and in exchange for a simple comment of gratitude: for example, tutorials on how play a certain song. By typing only the word "tutorial" in the YouTube search menu, for example, it is possible to find tens of thousands of videos made and uploaded by people with the aim of helping others on any subject. In addition, there are commercial applications to easily create tutorials; for example, the application that can be found at the site www.showme.com.

- Solve problems posed by others in thematic forums or elsewhere in order to provide potential assistance (we could say, to learn to teach) and in some cases interact with the same person who asked or another informant's responses (learning and explaining). Just typing a subject that interests us or asking a question in the section reserved by Google for debating forums yields a list of spaces where there is discussion on these issues.

- Gather at sites online, where, working cooperatively, they share and create new knowledge. The example of Wikipedia is well known. Sometimes we tend to see Wikipedia as an information resource, for many use it as such. But we should understand it here as the collaborative construction of knowledge, offering possibilities of improving what is known in order to teach it to others. Other examples could be the sites for specific games, "clans", and series media that are proliferating on the Internet. Sometimes, the passionate and cooperative work of the participants competes with commercial structures of reference, as in the case of the development of free software. Investigate the practices of amateur fansubbers, dedicated to translating and subtitling anime, which is then spread over the Internet. The teams (composed of translators, editors, compositors, coders, quality controllers and distributors) work more quickly and effectively than the professional industries and are able to distribute the subtitling of an episode less than 24 hours after its release in Japan. All this, without more reward than the broadcast of the episode and the experience of a team together in forums and chats.

All these forms of learning are based on networks of peers, and are characterized by their reciprocity. The participants feel that they can produce knowledge and culture, as well as evaluate it. In these contexts, contrary to activities driven by friendship, adults can participate and are seen – unlike teachers in formal contexts – as colleagues (not as authority figures), and in some cases as more experienced.

The participation of young people in the digital world is creating a gap not only between generations – as we noted on previous pages – but also, above all, between what young people do in their free time and what they do in schools or in formal teaching spaces. Information technology is intensive, and knowledge is being formatted not only online but also in our brains, unlike previous technologies (such as writing, maps, or the clock). This improves our ability to multitask, probably to the detriment of our capacity to think deeply and linearly, as we did before and which is still valued in school.

Nicholas Carr (2010) has collected evidence of how the Internet is changing our brains and our ways of thinking. The author warns that the network is developing low-level cognitive skills (design coordination, response reflections, visual processing), multitasking capacity (location, classification and rapid assessment) enabling multiple attention. All this sets up a different intelligence, where the capacity for attention and long-term memory, characteristic of humans, is entrusted to a machine. While we might think we are more intelligent than computers, we will become less so as computer technology advances. In any case, technologies are changing our brains, our minds, and, maybe even more important, the way we learn.

Some lessons from informal learning

We have stated that there is a gap between the informal forms of learning – today encouraged by digital technologies – and those proposed by institutions that constitute the formal spaces of education. The first are not only more effective, but also set up ways of thinking and learning often different from and conflicting with the ones traditionally proposed by schools.

How we can reduce that gap? How we can supplement both forms of learning to prevent their opposition?

a) Incorporating technologies to promote educational changes
    First of all, it seems necessary that the schools should have technologies that connect them to the digital world. But this does not mean flooding schools with computers or other gadgets, trusting that their mere presence will bring both fields closer. Practice on the introduction of digital textbooks (often a simple PDF of the paper versions), interactive whiteboards or individual laptops has not produced big changes in what and how things are taught (Marín, Barlam & Oliveres, 2011).

    As Monimó, Sigalés and Meneses (2008) argue, digital technologies are not the main innovative factor in the new forms of organizing practices in the network society, but merely a necessary tool to carry out the transformation that school education needs to respond to new social demands. In this regard, according to the authors, the introduction of such technologies should be accompanied by three challenges: create more efficient and productive processes of teaching and learning; change the forms of mediation, forcing a rethink of teaching procedures; and rethink the objectives of education.

    As a result, more than just introducing digital technologies, the key is a profound change in classrooms and schools to move them closer to effective ways of teaching and learning, some of whose components are well represented in informal learning. For example, when Carles Monereo (2005) proposes guidelines, we should bear in mind the educational uses of information and communications technology (ICT), many of which transcend mere technology: they are powerful guides for the improvement of school practice. Here are the guidelines listed in summary:

    • Educational objectives should guide the introduction of ICT and not vice versa.

- Face-to-face instruction is irreplaceable, so we must work towards a blended model.
- The use of ICT should be consistent with the concept of teaching and learning, acting in the process of negotiation of meanings rather than transmission of "truths".
- Prioritize socio-cognitive skills through interdisciplinary problem-solving and projects that enable ICT.
- Encourage active and collaborative involvement through planning peer-learning situations.
- Stimulate motivation and authentic problem-solving.
- Establish a system of effective and diverse support and scaffolding, identifying difficulties and providing tools for easy access via the Internet.
- Improve teaching by analysing progress and difficulties.
- Evaluate, giving priority to understanding and meaningful learning.
- Ensure respect for diversity and privacy, especially in interactions on the Web.

Thus, ICTs are not in themselves learning tools – they become that only if they are used to plan and regulate one's own and others' activity and psychological processes (Coll & Monereo, 2008). In this sense, ICT is an instrument of mediation between teacher and students or among the students themselves.

The psychologist Gordon Wells (1999), when formulating the guidelines for changes that should be undertaken in formal education to overcome the distance between it and informal education, never refers expressly to technology – as we say, it must be subject to the learning objectives. He indicates that teaching in schools and formal institutions should be oriented towards investigation and ensuring that issues and challenges that are being proposed to students connect with their interests, preferences and experiences. Teaching must use practices and mediatory tools which are potentially useful and recognize information and skill which is distributed among different members of the community. And, finally, it must create environments where all this will meet in a collaborative interaction.

b) Educate in participation in the uses of ICT
Second, after incorporating ICT, so that they help promote educational changes and facilitate accessibility to instruments and useful mediators, it is also unavoidable that the school teaches how to participate (Reig, 2012).

The use of ICT – inside and outside of school – must be accompanied by deliberate education in the digital tools and learning the new skills required. Thus, for example, in school children should be taught to read on the Internet (Cassany, 2011) and develop specific skills in digital reading, such as the formulation of the objectives of reading (for what do we seek information?); the use of search engines (with options of tuning and keywords); browsing through the network (with strategies to keep on course); and the assessment of the credibility of the consulted information (with recognition of authorship and purpose). In this same vein, use is increasingly growing of *Virtual Learning Environments* – such as the platform Moodle – that allows teachers and students to have a virtual classroom, with a multiplicity of resources at their disposal (email, forum, chat, wikis, blogs, links, associated files, etc.), to complete the face-to-face classroom.

c) Classrooms without walls

Third, we must consider that the walls of classrooms "fall" when we can connect to the Internet. Since the emergence of media, especially television, teachers have had to admit that they are not the only repositories of knowledge. This has had positive effects, not only for the incorporation of videos or audiovisual support in classrooms, but above all by the recognition of the loss of the monopoly and the opening of classrooms to experts of the environment (family, community members, etc.), or visits to it. Today classrooms are potentially connected with "out there", through the Internet – which allows not only the reception and use of many resources and instruments in classes, but also possibilities of learning by teaching other people beyond the classroom. In the next chapter we will see some examples.

d) Bridging formal and informal learning

Finally, the attempt to overcome the gap between the formal and the informal allowed testing initiatives between both spaces that built bridges or areas of intersection. For example, one of the proposals that erases the boundaries between formal and informal learning, between the classroom and leisure, is called *Personal Learning Environments* or PLEs (Adell & Castañeda, 2010). These are configured by the tools, content and people who are part of our social network of interests of learning and personal growth. We select our sources of information, interaction and construction of joint knowledge and build the PLE ourselves to define our interests. These technological environments are based on ubiquity (we can learn anywhere at any time), metacognition (becoming aware and reflecting on our learning), creativity (combining learning outcomes) and empowerment (self-regulated learning) (Jubany, 2012).

We can find other promising ideas for that change (Cobo & Moravec, 2011), which dilute the barrier between formal and informal learning and are based on peer learning and the opportunity to learn by teaching others. Let us look at three of them.

Peer 2 Peer University

Based on the idea of Peer to Peer or P2P (free and open exchange of content on the Internet), Peer 2 Peer University (P2PU) was founded in 2009 (http://p2pu.org/en/), under the theme "learning for all, about almost anything". It is a project of open education that seeks to organize learning outside the walls of traditional institutions, using the Internet and self-organization through peer learning. The university is composed of community (communication in the project space), courses (spaces to share knowledge with others), schools (discussion of specific thematic groups) and feed-back spaces (where learners write and evaluate proposals and courses).

As in any P2P system, the participants are volunteers, although the project receives donations from foundations and support from the University of California. Teachers are conceived as leaders or facilitators, without curricular requirements, under the premise that everyone can teach something. In fact, everyone is invited openly to participate in both the courses and discussion groups, suggest topics to create new ones, co-design them with the existing facilitators or propose a new one as a facilitator.

Course evaluations have highlighted as positive that in many courses participants (both students and teachers) come from formal institutions. Courses are evaluated by the participants, which offers facilitators learning opportunities about what they taught.

Bank of Common Knowledge

An example from practice and action of how the P2P model can be exported to non-digital spaces is the Bank of Common Knowledge (BCK), a project started by Platoniq (www.youcoop.org/) in 2006 as a laboratory of mutual education from citizen to citizen, or peer to peer. The name of Bank comes from the tradition and experience of other initiatives based on barter or LETS (Local Exchange Trading System), which have transcended the exchange of objects, giving rise to experiences like time banking. These practices are based on the principles of reciprocity, trust and mutual aid.

BCK adapted the techniques of networks for the exchange of files and the strategies of the free software movement to develop a new concept of education and peer-to-peer social organization, in which information is distributed across a network of volunteers, shareholders and donors. You can see a video summary at www.youtube.com/watch?v=5uOEVe9wy4c. Participation in BCK is open. You can be part of the organization and be a contributor, or generate offers and demands of knowledge and become an expert or donor. The proposal tries to blend knowledge that "donors" can share with the learning needs or requests of "shareholders". The face-to-face encounters between those who share knowledge and those who request it create spaces for knowledge sharing as a common good.

The BCK offers various teaching and learning formats:

* Demos, which provide information about how to do something, following certain steps. This format generates a manual, which responds to questions of "How…?"; for example, How do I make bread? How do I mount a server?
* Theory to carry: a set of interpretations is outlined on a concept or theme that helps you to understand it in its context. This may or may not have practical application. It answers questions of "What is…?": for example, What is cognitive capitalism? What are intellectual property rights?

- Experiences: explanations of processes and events. Transmitting experience can be useful or inspirational to other people in particular contexts. This format answers questions such as "How can this be solved?" or "How can I live in this situation?": for example, How do we denounce an illegal mobile phone antenna?
- Micro workshops: activities of co-learning, where participants work on a common task proposed by an expert: for example, a bicycle tuning workshop.
- Challenges: challenges test and measure knowledge, abilities or skills of experts and enthusiasts: for example, assembling a computer from parts in the shortest possible time.
- Games: non-competitive recreational activities which experiment with new forms of production, learning and participation on an equal footing. Games have proposals such as: What can we learn from a TV competition about managing collective decision-making? How do we understand the different effects of a production and collective distribution network, using only office material?

Knowledge exchanges are recorded to be published on the Internet and also invite and support the realization of capsules, which are videos that synthesize what is intended to be learned and which are available, subject to a license copy being left.

In the rapprochement between formal and informal learning, in this case with a learning idea of forms of sharing and building knowledge together in the Internet (through what the promoters of the project called "analogizing digital"), the BCK has also enabled practice in schools, which has given rise to experiences of expanded education where the students learn by teaching others.

Service-Learning

The Service-Learning initiative (Puig, 2009) comes more from the educational system. It is a form of experiential education in which students engage in activities that address human and community needs together with structured opportunities for reflection designed to achieve desired learning outcomes (Jacoby, 1996). Service-Learning has an international development, with a strong rooting in many Latin American countries (Centro Latinoamericano de Aprendizaje y Servicio Solidario www.clayss.org.ar/), and combines processes of learning and service to the community. It is a complex and well-articulated project, in which the participants learn by working on real needs in the environment with the aim of improving it. Service-learning is, therefore, an educational project with social utility.

The numerous experiences include varied activities, through which children and young people learn basic skills and curriculum content by offering a voluntary service in the community. For example, projects of recovery of the cultural and natural heritage; transmitting content through local media; and improving sustainability and solidarity-based initiatives. In many of these projects the principle of learning by teaching, although not usually explicitly in these terms, is very much present. Álvaro Ataz, a participating student in the Spanish Service-Learning Network, testifies:

"We teach computing to older people who had no idea. We had to prepare lessons, overcome the nerves at the beginning, relate to people who could be our grandparents. In addition, the experience of teaching them made us understand how teachers feel" (http://redaps.wordpress.com/que-es-el-aps/).

In other Service-Learning projects, however, there is deliberate use of the concept of learning by teaching to assure the learning of students who provide it. There is evidence of academic improvement for the students (Eyler, Giles & Dwight, 1999). An example is when American students of medicine learn anatomy by teaching the community (Montante, Nazar & Bee, 2013). We have to be attentive to these and many other interesting initiatives that are emerging every day, like the Shibuya University (www.shibuya-univ.net/english/), which proposes a university linked to lifelong learning, where people learn from one another from anywhere in the community.

Chapter 5

Learning by teaching in formal education

If you think about it a moment, the best way to learn something is to teach it. Then, why not have kids teaching other kids? How can we construct a context where that happens?
John Seely Brown (Chief Scientist of Xerox and Palo Alto Research Center, now co-Chairman of Deloitte Center of Edge; from "Tinkering as a mode of knowledge production": www.youtube.com/watch?v=9u-MczVpkUA)

In the previous chapters we have seen teaching as a specifically human activity which is more complex than its accompanying learning process. We have seen evidence of how teaching others can be a good learning mechanism for those who teach, especially when the teaching process takes place in bidirectional contexts. We have also seen how informal learning, the most abundant and effective form, offers us ways – encouraged by digital technologies – of peer learning and learning by teaching.

In this chapter we will focus on how formal education – developed mainly in schools, colleges and universities – incorporates learning by teaching into its practices, increasingly and deliberately: activities that embody the principle of learning by teaching, in an implicit or explicit way. These activities offer opportunities for students to learn by teaching their peers. To do this, in the first part of the chapter we will refer to the conceptual changes that are taking place in these formal contexts which support this type of initiative; and then, we will present examples of formal education practices containing the principle of learning by teaching.

In fact, there are many initiatives of this kind, although – as we shall see – not all of them explicitly recognize the learning of the student who teaches, while promoting it deliberately. We will present examples of these experiences with the aim of illustrating the initiatives and offer practical ideas for teachers. But certainly examples are just that, and teachers will be able to find other, richer examples that best suit individual contexts.

Finally, it is worth highlighting that learning by teaching practices should complement and enrich traditional forms of teaching in educational institutions, but not replace them. We are not conceiving of schools where students learn exclusively from their peers. We will say that the systematic implementation of these practices would enrich the quality of education of students and would allow the teacher to develop a new role, closer to that of facilitator and organizer of peer interactions.

Formal education in change

As we have seen in previous sections, social changes have generated huge amounts of pressure in educational systems, challenging them to respond to the new needs that our times demand of them. We often ask ourselves if we can educate the young in schools and tend to ask our educational systems to respond to all the social challenges, while keeping our minds still in the industrial idea of education, where school prepared us for life (Cobo & Moravec, 2011).

All the international reforms of educational systems take as a central axis the student-centred perspective, where the role of the teacher is not so much instruction – in the sense of transmitting information in a format of learning (Acaso, 2013) – but generating rich environments that promote the learning of the students, through processes that encourage active participation and autonomous work. In recent years, in these processes of change in educational systems, many elements in terms of the aims and forms of education have emerged which have much to do with the development of learning by teaching practices. We will review five of them.

The educational relevance of cooperation

Although traditionally classrooms and schools were organized around the individual and competitive learning, today we know that offering opportunities to students to cooperate and work together is absolutely necessary, for several reasons (Duran, 2009a).

- *Cooperation is a key competence for the knowledge society.* This is recognized by UNESCO (UNESCO, 1996) and by the OECD (DeSeCo, 2002). Therefore, it is not strange that cooperation and teamwork appear in listings of competences of all educational stages; or that being one of the main skills of the brain worker, business values it more each day and conceives it not only as a necessary employee competence, but also as a mechanism of inter-business development. The term "co-opetition" (Brandenburger & Nalebuff, 1998) combines the need to compete and cooperate. For competition, our educational systems work perfectly. The challenge still lies in cooperation.
- *Cooperation develops skills and attitudes needed for a democratic society.* Teamwork allows learners to play with skills and attitudes in real-life situations and develop interpersonal and cognitive skills useful to the argumentation of ideas, active listening to the views of others, the resolution of conflicts through negotiation and the assumption of shared agreements (Slavin, 1996). For example, cooperative learning is seen as an effective resource for intercultural education (Díaz-Aguado, 2005) and a necessary competence for the creation of a collective for social transformation (Perrenoud, 2001).
- *Cooperation is a significant learning engine.* As we have already seen, interactions with others allow us to create optimal conditions for the emergence of sociocognitive conflict (supported by the followers of the theories of Piaget) and necessary for the acting of the mediator (in terms of the theory of Vygotsky and his followers).

Learning is not an individual achievement, but rather the product of social activity with other, more experienced members offering assistance that allows the apprentice to become an ever more competent and autonomous participant (Wells, 1999). Being able to cooperate means being able to learn from each other and with the other, a competence that will allow us to learn throughout our lives.

• *Cooperative learning is an instructional strategy for quality education for all.* It allows the use of differences in knowledge between students, seeing diversity not as a problem but as an opportunity for learning (Stainback & Stainback, 1999). Thus, diversity within the team is a prerequisite for the establishment of relations of mutual aid, and we can also use differences in knowledge or skills so students can act as mediators in the construction of the knowledge of their peers (Duran, 2009b) – as we will see in the practices of the cooperative techniques and methods that follow in this chapter.

The instructional value of peer interactions

Traditionally schools considered that peer interactions had no educational value, and tried to minimize or discourage them. Take into consideration the traditional sentence "I will not speak in class". For whom was it intended? Not the teacher, of course, who was expected to use speech as a privileged instrument of knowledge construction. For the students? It depends. When students were questioned by the teacher, they were expected to respond instantly. The teacher–student interaction was valued. The sentence "I will not speak in class" was intended to apply to potential interactions between students, and deemed any talk between students as devoid of any educational value. Therefore, teachers were inclined to expel students who were talking, disregarding the possibility that one was helping the other.

Valuable interactions, in this point of view, were what went from the teacher to students. So the social organization of the class established only learning interactions between the teacher and students. This practice, which is still present in many classrooms where the teacher monopolizes the ability to teach, has had at least two consequences (Duran, 2007). First, it restricts potential sources of learning help to only one: the teacher, with whom the proportion of educational assistance available to each student is necessarily very limited (the aid *ratio*). But, in addition, aware of the educational needs of each one of our students, teachers tend to experience a sense of frustration for not being able to adjust teaching to each of their students.

Knowledge from the sciences of education and teaching are changing this initial situation. Today, more and more, peer interactions are seen as potential mechanisms of learning. We know that not all interaction between students drives learning, in the same way that not all interaction between the teacher and students does. But we openly recognize that students can learn among themselves, with conveniently organized interactions, and classrooms can become communities where the students learn not only from teacher support – always limited and little customizable – but also from the mutual aid offered (Baudrit, 2012).

In this sense, there are countless initiatives based in creative classrooms, understood as communities, where peer support is deliberately promoted and where students are taught the social skills necessary for offering and receiving aid (Sapon-Shavin, 1999). Thus, in many classrooms mutual aid is promoted through *Classroom Classifieds* or small ads where students communicate what they can teach (multiplication, rhythmic gymnastics, sign language, jumping rope, playing chess, playing the violin, etc.) and what they need by way of help (improving reading, using a computer programme, English, etc.). Students can also develop their own Yellow Pages, where they list the knowledge or skills that they may share or teach to their peers.

Canadian researchers Emma Van der Klift and Norman Kunc (1994) point out that our society – in general terms – has a dual view about who offers help and who requests it. Table 5.1 summarizes this idea. For people in need of help, like students with disabilities, it is not the help that awakens unsatisfactory feelings, but rather the loss of self-determination usually experienced by requesting it (creating dependency and the difficulty of deciding on the help itself).

But the paradox, according to the authors, is that in the school context and in the classroom in particular, things change radically. In the traditional context – characterized by the transmission of knowledge and individual and competitive learning – helping others is devalued. Often, students who help feel that they are doing something that is morally okay, but at the same time they experience a sense of loss of time and opportunities for their own learning through the imposition of an unwanted peer. Some families lament that their children "lose so much time" helping others, or even that children of other families lose their time helping theirs.

We, as teachers, might have contributed to this discrediting of peer support when we use it as a way of "levelling" time of execution of the tasks (making the fastest students help the slow ones so that all of them finish the activities at the same time) or when we use it as a form of support to students to whom we cannot attend, focusing our interest only on the assisted student and forgetting that – as is shown by our own teaching experience – the helper can learn by teaching.

Table 5.1 Social values of offering and receiving help

Dimension	Why we like to offer help	Why we dislike to be helped
Skill	It reaffirms the ability	It implies deficiency
Value	It reaffirms value	It means to be a burden
Position	It reaffirms the superiority	It implies inferiority
Obligation	By duty	By obligation
Vulnerability	Hides it	Reminds us

Source: Adapted from Van der Klift & Kunc, 1994.

Van der Klift and Kunc (1994) propose to place mutual help in the centre of learning interactions: support for empathy (recognizing that we all need to be helped); making the help as reciprocal as possible (all can help and be helped); and not forcing the friendship (help is not the same as being friends). Creating awareness in the student who pedagogically helps others that this activity can be a good opportunity for their own learning is certainly the best way to make sense and give prestige to peer support. But to do that, we need to turn peer support into peer learning. That means organizing – or structuring – this helping relationship with the express purpose that the person who helps can also learn (Topping, Buchs, Duran & Van Keer, 2017).

Turn peer interactions into peer learning

Topping (2005) identified the main processes that can lead to the realization of effectiveness in peer learning, in which interactive dialogue is responsible for the negotiation of meaning, which promotes shared self-regulation and processes which scaffold help in a framework of intersubjectivity. This co-construction of knowledge, however, does not occur spontaneously, but requires careful planning.

We all know that it is not enough to organize students in groups and wait for cooperation to magically arise. On the contrary, simple group work is characterized by the dissipation of responsibilities and the fact that one student works to compensate for – or sometimes impede – the work of others, while others contribute less or nothing. It is necessary that the teacher structures interaction within the group to stimulate the emergence of cooperation.

Imagine a football coach encouraging his players onto the field with the slogan "Here you have the ball and there is the goal. Put it in as many times as you can ... Ah, but remember: do it as a team!" We know what would happen. Conversely, the good coach distributes roles amongst players, and creates actions and interactions between members, in which individuals are often subject to the interest of the team. The group becomes a team and knows that it is the team who wins or loses, not its members separately. How many times do teachers give a task to students – sometimes even tasks that can be solved individually – organize them in groups and remind them "Ah, but remember: do it as a team!"? And how many times are we bothered because some do nothing and others do all the work?

In order to overcome the problems of the simplistic working group, and turn it into real team or cooperative work, the teacher must arrange interactions between members of the team in such a way that yields compliance with the five principles proposed by David and Roger Johnson from the University of Minnesota (2008).

These principles, refined by other authors (like Kagan and Kagan, 2009), are widely accepted by the scientific community. We will review them in summary, since they guide the actions of the teacher in promoting cooperative learning.

1   *Positive interdependence.* The success of each member is connected to the rest of the team, and vice versa. This is established through the objectives of the team (learn and make sure that the rest of the team members also learn), group

recognition (the reinforcement is not individual, but team), division of resources (distribution of information and limitation of materials) and complementary roles.

2 *Individual accountability and personal responsibility.* This tries to minimize or avoid the main drawback of teamwork: the diffusion of responsibilities, reflected in the student who contributes little or nothing ("loafing effect") or the student who does the work of others (the others would be "free riders"). To ensure accountability, individual assessment and the random choice of a spokesperson or personal work reports are recommended.

3 *Promotive interaction.* Maximize opportunities for interaction that foster interpersonal dynamics of help, assistance, support, animation and reinforcement between the team members. This involves limiting the number of members per group and encouraging resource sharing, confidence, motivation, feedback and decision making. This element embraces face-to-face interactions but also virtual interactions, which are more and more common in *Computer Supported Collaborative Learning* (Koschmann, 1996; Vinagre, 2010).

4 *Appropriate use of social skills.* The skills necessary for cooperation (knowing and trusting others, proper communication, acceptance and support for others and constructive resolution of conflicts) have to be deliberately taught so that they can put into practice.

5 *Group processing.* The members of the team should spend some time reflecting together on the effectiveness with which members carry out the process to achieve the team objectives, and on the working relationships, and make decisions for readjustment and improvement.

In order to help structure the interaction within the groups, turning them into teams, there have arisen so-called *cooperative structures*: didactic designs, some more complex than others, which, following the above conditions, promote cooperation through organizational proposals which are free of content. The speed with which willingness to practise cooperative learning has spread has led to the creation and development of many of these structures which, while sharing to a greater or lesser degree the above-mentioned principles, constitute a rich universe, but one which is complex and difficult to classify (Duran & Monereo, 2012; Topping, Buchs, Duran & Van Keer, 2017).

In general, we can divide cooperative structures into methods and techniques. We define methods as complex and sophisticated structures that often require more time and initial training of students, making it advisable to use these structures if the peer learning is to be regular. On the other hand, techniques are simple structures that can be applied with simple steps, without initial training, creating what could be called a few minutes of cooperative learning in the classroom. In Johnson and Johnson's terms (1990), methods can be understood as formal cooperative learning and techniques as informal.

The differences between these methods and techniques are so great that some authors are beginning to point out that we cannot refer to cooperative learning as a single entity, but rather should speak based on these methods and specific techniques, each of which has a target and effect different from the other (Sharan, 2010).

A challenge: share teaching with our students

Johnson and Johnson (2008) argue that learning cooperatively is one of the more studied topics in the psychology of education, in all the stages and areas of curriculum. Meta-analyses of research conclude that cooperative learning in general improves academic performance and attitudes towards learning, and this applies across very different subjects (Johnson & Johnson, 1990; Slavin, 1996; Springer, Stanne & Donovan, 1999; Johnson, Johnson & Smith, 2007).

But despite it being recognized and supported by research, the use of cooperative learning in the classroom is not an easy task at first. There are difficulties that must be taken into consideration, thinking about how to overcome them, and teachers must be able to incorporate this methodology in the usual procedure for teachers and schools, turning classrooms into communities of learners, where students learn not only from the teacher, but also from the mutual help offered by peers under the umbrella of teacher organization and monitoring.

Among these difficulties, some authors point out individualism rooted among students, the lack of teacher preparation time and support, or that the families and society have a mentality focused on only some learning contents (Lobato, 1998). Some others added the "Taylorist" school organization (Rué, 1998) or noted the main mistakes made when teachers start using cooperative learning in their classrooms (Grisham & Molinelli, 2001). They make oversized and over-homogeneous teams; there are not enough explicit instructions; they do not give enough time for interaction; there is too much physical distance between team members; often there is ill-structured activity (involving little interdependence or individual participation); teams are changed before problems are resolved; often social skills are not taught or monitored consistently; they do not give time or guidelines for team self-assessment; they do not look at what doesn't work (only at what is working); they use teams infrequently; or they evaluate complex cooperative work too soon.

It seems essential that, in a traditional school based on individual and competitive learning, the inclusion of peer learning requires not only the recognition of cooperation as a basic competence at all educational levels, but also making organizational decisions necessary, starting with the physical furniture and difficulties of having appropriate spaces (Guilmette, 2007) and ending with teacher training in the use and implications of peer learning (Boud, Cohen & Sampson, 2001).

This last aspect which seems central is the need to replace the obsolete conception of teaching and learning, based on a transmissive idea of knowledge monopolized by the teacher, with a new conception where the teacher provides assistance and organizes mutual help among the students, helping them promote their own knowledge construction. It means that teachers must recognize *that students can teach* their peers (and learn by teaching), if opportunities and support are given to them. With teachers having lost the monopoly of knowledge, given its being distributed among people and through the Internet, it is now time to share with our students the latest monopoly we have: the ability to teach.

Are we willing to do so? If we do, we will achieve a far more democratic class-room with more sources of pedagogical assistance available for learning.

The emergence of a new competence: learning to teach

The deliberate use of situations in which students learn through teaching their peers will be accompanied by the growing explicit recognition of this principle and by providing teacher help and support to enable students to perform the complex task of teaching effectively. In real situations that are exemplified below, in many of these initiatives peer tutors receive initial or additional training on how to perform their role, and especially how to teach. In other cases, teachers offer models for instruction and, on many occasions, technical or educational resources. In addition, peer tutors often receive continuous feedback from the tutees or the teachers about their teaching performance; and, finally, the quality of pedagogical support they have offered is also evaluated.

All this is, no doubt, a real process of learning how to teach. Students who have opportunities for learning by teaching and receiving this type of support are learning to teach. For example, considering that teaching forms part of the role of nurses, the Monash University in Australia has a programme through which, before graduation, students teach laboratory techniques to novice students, with the deliberate purpose of learning to teach (McKenna & French, 2011).

If this competence, teaching, was recognized and even evaluated (as it already is in many of the practices that we discuss), we would be faced with the emergence of a new competence which, as we have maintained throughout these pages, would help to build a sustainable and democratic knowledge society, where we all learn from everyone (and we all teach everyone).

Formal situations of students who learn by teaching

There is a rich and growing universe of school practices that include the principle of learning by teaching, although not always explicitly. In our view, there are no practices *of* learning teaching, as if it were a pedagogical method. Rather, there are rich and complementary practices that teachers use which include this principle. We will see, then, examples of situations in which teachers have shared with their students the ability to teach, encouraging them to learn by teaching their peers.

Learning by developing educational materials

As we have seen in Chapter 3, a first way into learning by teaching is to prepare an explanation without giving it. This can materialize into learning to present it through didactic material that allows others to learn it. Eric Marcos, a math teacher at Lincoln Middle School in Santa Monica (California), suggests that students learn how to develop video tutorials. He tells us (www.youtube.com/watch?v=_8OAfHg0CP4)

that, in answer to an email from a student, he started to prepare a video to explain a math concept with his tablet. He recorded his explanation and wrote on the screen (just as he would do in class with a blackboard). Then he realized that that same explanation passed to other students would be found helpful. And soon Marcos and his students established a website to lodge that and other videos. In a short time, students began to produce video tutorials. Now, that website – called Mathtrain-tv (http://mathtrain.tv) – can be consulted, so that students not only learn by making such explanations, they also offer opportunities for others to learn through making videos. Not only can other students in the class learn, but students from other schools anywhere in the world can also learn.

In an interesting study about the experience (November, 2012), Marcos's students recognize that "to make a good tutorial, you must really learn math". With a relatively simple technological system and software within the reach of everyone, students have the opportunity to make a video of a few minutes. The process of making the video, although simple, is innovative and creative, since the students bring into play their imagination to make an attractive and clear explanation. This develops the student's sense of control, autonomy, skilfulness and purpose (and yields an authentic product with a real audience). All this has an impact, no doubt, on students' motivation. While they were making the videos, the teacher could see how his students redefined the ideas and identified learning difficulties and ways to address them.

Although we have the phenomenon of expectancy (students learn to teach, but in fact they do not interact with their potential trainees), the website logs visits and allows rating of the videos and the leaving of messages. At the end of all the videos, the student author says they are grateful we have watched his or her video.

In another geographical context, in the University of León (Spain) engineering students developed several videos of a maximum of ten minutes, about different topics of topography (Álvarez, Rodríguez-Pérez, Sanz-Ablanedo & Fernández-Martínez, 2008). Videos, created this time in teams, were placed on the Internet to be available to students who needed to learn these topics.

Evaluation of this experience reported improvement in participating students with respect to their cognitive abilities, methodological skills (organization, decision-making and problem-solving), technological skills (ICT and information management) and language skills (oral and written communication and rigorous use of technical language). In addition, improvements were detected in critical and self-critical skills, transmission of opinions and social skills relating to social interaction and cooperation.

Learning by replacing the teacher in front of a group

Even though in all education levels we can find practices in which students replace some of the functions of the teacher, it is in higher education that this is documented more substantially. In the 1970s in the United States, there was published a review of experiences of *peer teaching* at the university level (Goldschmid & Goldschmid, 1976). This identified discussion groups, led by the teacher's student assistants, who, having studied the subject previously, helped student groups to discuss activities and to prepare for exams, corrected by themselves. Although the concept was already reported at that time as *To Teach Is to Learn Twice* (Whitman, 1988), the focus was on the student apprentices, and the assistant student was seen as something of a substitute for the teacher.

Thus, this type of initiative is perhaps better described as *Surrogate Teaching*, in which functions of the teacher are delegated to students, like grading exams, monitoring written works or discussing with groups (Goodlad & Hirst, 1989). Even so, many of those practices, which sometimes were rewarding even outside the curriculum, have been gradually incorporated into curricular activities, and the work of the student assistant has been valued from the perspective of their own learning. So, to give a concrete example, in the Faculty of Medicine of the University of Michigan, fourth-year students learn to recognize cultural diversity by teaching it to groups of 10 or 12 students in the second year (Tang, Hernandez & Adams, 2004).

Preparing a lesson for the rest of the class group is the basis of the so-called model LdL (*Lernen durch Lehren* or learning by teaching), developed by the Professor of Didactics of French Jean-Pol Martin (see www.Ldl.de). In order to overcome the short time for oral expression in traditional teaching of second-language students, it was suggested that they should adopt the role of teacher, preparing and teaching a class on previously determined content. The purpose was that the student learned to teach not only curriculum content (grammar, for example) and communicative competence, but also complex thinking skills associated with teaching (Grzega & Schöner, 2008).

In the same area we find practices in universities in which students support the tutorial work of teachers, although this can look more like peer mentoring. In general, advanced students (of higher grades) take advantage of their experience and receive training, in many cases, and provide support to small groups of novice students, accompanying them in the process of incorporation into the institution and helping them to clarify objectives, achieve goals, resolve doubts, improve learning and solve problems.

Many experiences come from English-speaking universities, but universities working in other languages – Spanish, for instance – have valuable proposals which increasingly focus on advanced student learning (Duran & Flores, 2015). A well-known proposal is that of the University of la Laguna (Álvarez & Gonzalez, 2007). Other experiences include that of the Autonomous University of Barcelona (Chancel, Jordana & Pericon, 2008) and the peer tutoring programme at the University of Granada (Fernandez & Arco, 2011). In many cases, such as at the Universidad de la República in Uruguay (Mosca & Santiviago, 2010), these initiatives are widespread to different degrees and fully embedded in the institutional methodological repertoire.

Although originally all these initiatives sought to complement teacher action by putting the experience of students in motion, increasingly they have become concerned about what the tutor is learning, training them for this purpose and recognizing curricular learning. All these approaches are within the scope of peer tutoring, which we will address shortly. In these projects mentioned above, generally the tutor acts with a small group.

Learning by teaching through cooperative learning techniques

As already mentioned, in order for peer interaction to give learning opportunities, it must be suitably structured. This is why we can use cooperative structures, which we have divided into techniques – simple structures, which some authors also call informal cooperative learning – and methods, which are more complex structures. We will focus now on the first.

Techniques establish clearly what students should do (and not do) at any time; they speak to the achievement of concrete and short-term goals; they activate very well-defined cognitive processes; they are of short duration (from a few minutes to a maximum of an hour session); they require a relatively low level of cooperative skills, thanks to the dynamic; and they refer to small and sporadic groups (pairs, trios, quartets). These characteristics make them a suitable way to begin to use cooperative learning in the classroom and to proceed to articulate more complex dynamics from a combination of some of them (Varas & Zariquiey, 2011).

There are many cooperative learning techniques, and they are simple and versatile. Spencer Kagan presents more than 140 (Kagan & Kagan, 2009). So it is not that educators know all of them – an impossible mission – but that, from knowing and using some of them, teachers understand well the cooperative principles on which they rest, and can develop their own techniques spontaneously. Knowing these principles, teachers can select the techniques that best meet their needs and adjust, combine or reinvent them (Pujolàs, 2008).

We will look at four examples of techniques of cooperative learning, all showing ease of use in the classroom (Duran, 2012).

* *Active knowledge sharing* (Silberman, 1996)
    Before a presentation or new information, the teacher formulates a series of questions that are part of the knowledge to come (for example: terms, persons or pictures to identify, facts or concepts). In pairs, students try to answer the questions. They can get up and resort to other pairs to complete their answers. All students have the opportunity to activate their prior knowledge and begin to compare it – to actually start learning from their peers.
* *Think-pair-share* (Lyman, 1992)
    In the course of an explanation, the teacher poses a question (to check understanding, investigate application, meet doubts, etc.). The teacher gives students a short time to think individually (they can write the answer) and then, with their peer, discuss ideas that are shared with the rest of the class. It is a very effective technique to keep the attention of students and is an opportunity to reason and discuss the topic, with students starting to teach their own reasoning and improve it with the contribution of the other. It allows, in addition, the rehearsal of a response before submitting it to the group. There is an example of this

technique in a math class in primary school at www.teachingchannel.org/videos/think-pair-share-lesson-idea.

A variant of this same technique is *peer instruction*, developed and evaluated at Harvard University. After a short presentation, the teacher presents a conceptual question, students argue for two or three minutes and then compare their responses with the response of the teacher (Crouch & Mazur, 2001).

- *Numbered heads together* (Kagan, 1992)

  Each team member has a number from 1 to 4 (for teams of four students). The teacher proposes an activity for the teams, and its members must work together to resolve it and make sure that all the teammates understand it well. Later, the teacher requests that students with a particular number – which is determined randomly – explain how they have solved the task. The provision of pedagogical mutual assistance among the members of the team – who will teach each other – is promoted, as they do not know which of them will have to explain the activity in front of the class group.

- *Structuring academic controversy* (Johnson & Johnson, 1994)

  Two pairs of students operate in teams of four. They seek information or evidence to argue a certain position. Each pair gathers evidence in opposite directions. The teacher can offer resources – texts, dossiers, data, and so on – for each position. Once each team is prepared, each pair presents its position with the arguments in favour. Later, pairs exchange their position and select the arguments targeted by the other pair that they want to develop or enhance. Finally, the four members of the team make a synthesis of the best arguments from both points of view, learning and teaching each other and developing the perspectives and empathy. As we have said, techniques of cooperative learning promote work in teams made up quickly for the occasion, with episodes of learning by teaching in short spaces of time within the same class.

Learning by teaching through cooperative learning methods

We have defined cooperative learning methods as complex structures which require initial training of students for their use. They usually go beyond the short times of techniques, and can extend their work over several sessions or classes.

This feature of greater sophistication of cooperative learning methods has, in our view, two consequences. On the one hand, it is not so much applying the techniques directly, step by step, but more putting them into practice in an appropriate way, taking the teacher's own educational context and objectives into account. No one knows the classroom better than the teacher does. Methods require decisions to adapt them to the local context, and success depends largely on the quality of such decisions. Knowing that cooperative learning methods are nothing more than teaching designs, some more complex than others, it is crucial that the teacher knows the underlying principles and decides which methods to use and how to adjust, re-create or reinvent them, depending on the teacher's educational interests.

Second, if teachers require students to learn how to use these principles, both the teacher and the students (with initial training) will find it well worth using them regularly in order to benefit from the practice. It should be recalled that when we use cooperative learning methods, students not only cooperate to learn, but also learn to cooperate – and that learning is complex and demands continuing practice. Teamwork requires the development of many complex social skills involving working with others (active listening, empathy, the negotiation of agreements, etc.). We can say that, like cycling, we learn to cooperate to cooperate to learn. It is paradoxical that when a teacher confesses to avoiding the use of the word "teamwork" with his or her students, the students do not know how to work as a team. Precisely, if they do not know, we should give them opportunities for working together so that they can learn.

From the many cooperative learning methods, we will mention then only three, highlighting the potential of learning by teaching.

Jigsaw (Aronson & Patnoe, 2011 and Slavin, 1995)

Without doubt the *Jigsaw*, initially created by Elliot Aronson, is the best-known cooperative learning method. Knowing that a way of creating positive interdependence and promoting individual responsibility – essential characteristics of cooperation – is to distribute information or knowledge among the different members of the team, Aronson devised the *Jigsaw Classroom*.

The proposal arose in the classrooms of the University of Texas in 1971, the first year that students from different ethnic groups shared the class after the abolition of racial segregation. The organization of the class – so that each student can be essential and valuable – was intended to help to overcome racial conflict and improve the learning of all students. You can read the beginning of this proposal – including a letter from a student ten years later – on the website of the University of California (www.jigsaw.org). Aronson intended that every student in the class had a piece of the puzzle – a portion of the knowledge necessary to complete the lesson objective. The difficulty was that each piece needed to be unique, independent and make sense in itself, which was only possible in the classes of very few students.

From this evocative idea, the education psychologist Robert Slavin developed *Jigsaw II*, creating small teams of about four people. The procedure was as follows:

- Base team: Students are organized in heterogeneous teams, where each member must learn a part of the knowledge necessary to reach the objective of the team. For example, if the lesson objective is to learn about different kinds of alternative energy to decide which is the more suitable in a given context, the teacher distributes one of those energies to each member of the team. At the same time, one student will be expert in solar energy, the other in wind, the other in tidal and the other in geothermal. They know that they will learn something that their peers are unaware of and will need. Each one will become an expert in one section.

- Groups of experts: To become "experts", the students of different base teams that share the same part of the knowledge gather in groups, where they will solve some activities to enhance the knowledge in question. Here they further learn their piece of the puzzle, which they will then have to teach to their teammates. For primary school pupils, it should be convenient to offer time and help so that students can create educational materials supporting their explanations and even rehearse them before returning to the team base.
- Back to the team base: Each expert returns to his or her team, where they should contribute their piece of knowledge necessary to achieve the overall learning objective. Each team member must, therefore, teach the others. All contributions are equally valuable and necessary, and students must not only take responsibility for their own learning (of their piece of the puzzle and understanding that of others), but they are also responsible for their teammates' learning, helping everyone to understand the different parts, without which no-one can learn successfully or follow the evaluation activity.

Despite the triple sequence team–group of experts–team, *Jigsaw* is relatively simple and very versatile. In fact, it is fragmenting the objective in as many parts as there are members in the teams (or even creating teams with as many members as there are parts in the objective). This makes it very powerful and practical for any area of knowledge.

There are different variations of the *Jigsaw* method. One of them is the *students teams achievement division*, designed by Slavin (1978), which eliminates the phase of work in the group of experts, making students learn their part individually and then teach it to their teammates. Another is *Teaming*, designed by Dentler (1994), in which members of the team double their opportunities of teaching, sharing their piece of the puzzle not only once (with all members of their team), but first in pairs and then in two pairs. In all these situations, episodes of learning by teaching in all the different ways (expectancy, explaining, interacting) are clearly present.

Reciprocal teaching (Palincsar & Brown, 1984)

Anne-Marie Palincsar and Ann Brown devised *reciprocal teaching* to develop reading comprehension. It involves distributing the cognitive functions that an expert reader performs (read and summarize, question, answer, anticipate) among the members of the team. Each team member has a role corresponding to one of these mental functions: the first to read and summarize; the second, question; the third, responding; and the last, anticipate. So, the cognitive functions that simultaneously make up the mind of an expert are distributed among different minds which are sharing the cognitive load and working cooperatively, turning those functions in roles. *Reciprocal teaching* is a cooperative learning method with good research (Rosenshine & Meister, 1994).

These mental functions, now roles, can rotate, along with text fragments or in different sessions. The cognitive load distribution allows the team members to view these procedures that otherwise go unnoticed because some students have not acquired them yet (think of children who are learning to read) or because they have already automated them and they have become unconscious. The support that team members offer playing their role not only allows them to confront complex texts – that students would not be able to understand without their teammates' help – but also to learn these procedures (internalize them) and use them independently when making individual readings (Palincsar & Brown, 2009).

Reading comprehension procedures are learned by teaching teammates or are taught by teammates. Distributing mental functions for the achievement of a task between different members of a team, in the form of roles, creates positive interdependence which can easily be transferred to other academic activities. For example, it would be sufficient to identify which mental functions develop in an expert and distribute them among the members of the team to generate collaborative writing or mathematical problem-solving methods.

Group investigation (Sharan & Sharan, 1994)

Going back to the work of John Dewey, the American psychologist considered a father of progressive education, Yael and Shlomo Sharan (1994) devised this method that considers the class as a scientific community, organized in teams, working for the achievement of a common educational goal or theme, but where each team works on a subtopic. Thus, for example, all the class is working on the same topic or teaching objective (e.g. the health consequences of drug use), but each team chooses a subtopic or reaches the target for different content (so that one team is working on the subject of alcohol, another of designer drugs, another of heroin, etc.). Students emulate the scientists who research subtopics within a common theme. Each team is organized autonomously, according to a plan of work from the teacher. The role of the teacher is organizing, monitoring activities and distributing tasks and responsibilities to ensure positive interdependence. Following the scientific metaphor, the activity ends by pulling the results of each team together.

As you can see, this team research group is very close to other interesting practices in educational contexts, related to what is called project-based learning (you can watch a good presentation at www.youtube.com/watch?v=LMCZvGesRz8). Projects in primary school (Algás et al., 2010) or secondary school (Departament d'Ensenyament, 2010) are practices that this method can complement and enrich. Teams teach the rest of the class what they have learned. Many of these practices take advantage of presentations, so that the other teams formulate questions and assess – through peer assessment – the level of achievement of the objective as well as the quality of the explanation.

Peer tutoring: students learning by teaching others

Keith Topping argues that peer tutoring has gone beyond archaic views – which portrayed the student tutor as a substitute for the teacher, helping tutees to learn – and can be defined as people of similar social groups who help others and themselves learn by teaching (Topping, 2000). As we saw in Chapter 3, the first evidence of learning by teaching came from the use of peer tutoring in schools, leading teachers to discover that tutors learned even more than their own tutees. In the school context, peer tutoring could be understood as a peer learning method based on the creation of pairs, with an asymmetrical relationship, with tasks for the respective roles: tutor and tutee. Both students have a common and shared objective, which is the acquisition or improvement of some curricular competence, through structured interactions planned by the teacher (Duran & Vidal, 2004).

Both these definitions move away from simple work in pairs, with a most able student helping one less able, since they require planning of interaction between both members, so that the student tutor learns by teaching and the tutee also learns in receiving personalized help from his or her tutor. *Peer tutoring* is being widely used in many countries, at all educational levels and curricular areas, and it is recommended by experts in education – such as the European Agency for Special Education and UNESCO – as a highly effective practice for inclusive education. The potential of one-to-one contact allows some authors to place it among the top ten most effective practices (Walberg & Paik, 2000).

We can find peer tutoring experiences between students of different ages (known as *cross-age tutoring*) in which the student tutor is the older one, or between students of the same age (known as *same-age tutoring)*, with fewer organizational complications in schools. According to whether the roles are fixed or interchangeable, we can distinguish between *fixed role* and *reciprocal* tutoring (Topping, Duran & Van Keer, 2016).

Peer tutoring practices are not new (Topping, 2015). Teachers have been using them in small rural schools, for example, with their single classroom of students of different ages, and have used these differences to help the younger children. But what now needed is to create formats of interaction in which both students learn, not only the tutee. If only tutees learn, thanks to the personalized and permanent support that they receive from the tutor, it would result in a bad methodology: only half the students of a class organized in pairs would be learning.

In order to promote tutor learning, it is necessary to carefully plan the interaction in the pair, designing a relationship between tutor and tutee to allow for the tutor to learn by teaching. As we saw in Chapter 2, this happens because the tutors prepare materials (creating teaching material for their tutees), are active in the interaction with their tutees and assume challenges that carry them beyond what they already know (their zone of proximal *teaching*).

An example in primary education is *Reading in Pairs*, a programme for the improvement of reading competence (Duran, Flores, Oller, Thomson-Garay & Vera, 2016). It is a set of materials to help schools use this methodology, deploying differences – in this case in linguistic competence – as a source of learning. Organized in pairs, tutors (a little more skilful) learn by teaching, and tutees learn thanks to the personalized help received. The interaction is highly structured, so that both members of the pair receiving initial training know at all times what is expected of them. Schools also offer initial training to families, who are encouraged to act as reading tutors of their sons and daughters at home (Blanch, Duran, Valdebenito & Flores, 2013).

After initial training, the programme develops in 24 half-hour sessions, twice a week, of reading in the classroom and often with other reading at home. During the sessions *activity sheets*, which contain texts from the actual environment of students and comprehension questions, structure the interaction in the pairs. The sessions consist of the folllowing:

1   Prior reading activities: involving various strategies (reading, activation of prior knowledge and elaboration of hypotheses).
2   Reading aloud: the tutor reads the text as a model, then both read aloud at the same time, then the tutee reads and the tutor uses *pause, prompt and praise*, an effective reading-in-pairs technique (Burns, 2006). While the tutee reads aloud, the tutor is listening carefully and when the tutee makes a mistake, the tutor takes a *pause*. After a few seconds, if the error is not corrected by the tutee, the tutor offers a *prompt* – or more than one, if necessary – and finally tutors *praise* the tutee for getting the correct answer.
3   Text comprehension: involving checking initial hypotheses, identifying the main ideas and formulating and resolving questions of comprehension of all types (literal, reorganization and synthesis, inference and deep or critical understanding).
4   Expressive reading by tutee: in addition, every four sessions pairs perform a self-assessment, reflecting and reviewing their progress. This metacognitive reflection allows them to consider goals of improvement for the following sessions.

Results of research in different languages show improvement for both tutors and tutees in fluency and reading comprehension (Flores & Duran, 2013; Valdebenito & Duran, 2013). But in some cases, like the development of the reader's self-concept, the best result is for the tutors, who have learned by teaching (Flores & Duran, 2015). Beyond this specific example, many other good practices exist, many of them backed by research in a large number of curriculum areas and at various levels of formal education (Topping, Duran & Van Keer, 2016).

Peer assessment: learning to correct and providing feedback

Offering students opportunities to evaluate their peers (and be evaluated by their peers) can also be a good way to learn from the other and from oneself, contrasting and reflecting on how others have solved the same activity, learning from one's mistakes and offering feedback for improvement. Thus, *peer assessment* is considered to be a form of peer learning (O'Donnell & Topping, 1998). When students have the opportunity of learning to assess their peers, the activity of evaluation is placed within the same sequence of teaching and learning.

When teachers take home piles of work to correct, following the system which prescribes that we are the only ones qualified to evaluate, students are excluded from that process. The only thing that we allow them is receiving a little weak feedback (a mark or a brief qualitative comment in the best of cases). Then, instead of taking so much homework, why do we not share with our students the criteria for correction and distribute the work among them?

Peer assessment is one of the strategies that most help self-regulation (Sanmartí, 2007), helping students to make conscious decisions about the strategies used to achieve a goal, monitor progress and evaluate the level of achievement. As a consequence, a key element is the explication of the correction criteria. The teacher should facilitate developing these criteria with the help of the assessing students (in the form of evaluation rubrics, for example) and argue about them. The clarification of the evaluation criteria, especially if they have been negotiated, facilitates more comprehensive learning. Furthermore, a careful reading of the peer text allows assessors to identify ways of thinking differently, to acknowledge mistakes and contrast other productions with their own. Whenever we use this practice with our students, at the end we ask if it has been useful. Some of the students openly acknowledge that they have learned more during the peer assessment – especially understanding the criteria of correction – than when they did the original work (Duran & Blanch, 2007).

Offering students the chance to assess their peers also allows them to learn to evaluate, a necessary competence for developing autonomous students. Daniel Cassany, a language didactics professors, holds that "someday we will all will have to become editors of our texts, when there is no teacher in front that can correct them" (Cassany, 1993, p48).

In fact, our students' sharing correction of works in the form of self or peer assessment can improve the quality of our own assessment. First, because it allows students more time to carefully evaluate their work. It is much more efficient when the classroom is arranged so that each student corrects the work of another. And second, because of having necessarily explicit evaluation criteria – that must be shared with the students, presented to them, argued with them and, if possible, negotiated with them – helps us as teachers to improve the quality of the assessment. Reviews of research on peer assessment (Topping, 1998; Falchikov & Goldfinch, 2000) show that its effectiveness depends, largely, on clarity and understanding of the evaluation criteria.

Perhaps some of the reluctance of teachers to share correction with students comes from the suspicion that students will help each other. Neither research nor experience confirms this supposition. Most students tend to be demanding, maybe more so than the teacher. Again, the way to correct one or another trend is through sharing the criteria for correction. As Nancy Falchikov says, the "agreement between student and teacher marks may not be the most important aspect of successful self- or peer assessment. Real success should follow from the enhancement of student learning that results from participation in the process" (Falchikov, 2001, p272).

Even so, for the peace of our own minds and that of our students, teachers can occasionally revise peer corrections. A practical procedure, once students have corrected the work of a peer, is to return the work to the author to review the peer corrections and, if necessary, express disagreement on the assessment of an item, arguing why in relation to the rubric or correction criteria. The teacher can then check these discrepancies. Peer review helps teachers release time in the correction process, allowing them to focus attention on the most problematic or unusual cases.

Finally, peer assessment opens the door to *feedback* processes through which students can receive relevant information to improve their work (Boud & Molloy, 2013). The assessor students have the time to offer this detailed help to their peers, which constitutes constructive aid – within the ZPD of their peers – acting as a guide to improve the work.

It is clear that not all forms of feedback are equally effective (Topping, 2010), and that it is necessary to train assessors to offer clues, more than correct or constructed answers, so that their peers can improve through responding to these cues. This activity of choosing the level of aid allows students – in their role as assessors – to be constructing reflective knowledge, and consequently to learn by teaching (Topping, Dehkinet, Blanch, Corcelles & Duran, 2013).

Teachers and students co-teaching

Co-teaching could be defined as two or more people sharing a classroom group instructional responsibility (Villa, Thousand & Nevin, 2008). The possibility of two teachers sharing teaching in the same class is one of the proposals from the school reform movement towards inclusive education, to create classes and schools able to respond to the needs of all students, regardless of their characteristics. *Co-teaching* offers better possibilities of giving attention, especially to students with special needs (Huguet, 2009), and in turn creates conditions so that teachers can learn from one another and thus improve their teaching practices (Rytivaara & Kershner, 2012).

In several countries, like the United States, the educational administration has suggested that support teachers co-teach with general teachers, both dealing with students at risk of exclusion, as well as offering support to teachers to improve their methodologies. In the United States, the existence of co-teaching practices together with the growing use of peer learning has allowed the emergence of a new form of co-teaching: students acting as co-teachers. Richard Villa, Jacqueline Thousand and Ann Nevin (2010) described co-teaching with students as an avant-garde initiative that goes ahead of research. Even so, it is important to include it in this section, because it demonstrates the dynamic nature of a school's practices of learning by teaching. If, in some of the initiatives we mentioned above, the student replaced the teacher (or any of the teacher's functions), this is clearly using the teaching as learning mechanism.

From interesting practices reported in two California secondary schools, Nevin, Villa and Thousand propose four forms of co-teaching.

* *Supportive co-teaching.* One co-teacher – the teacher – takes the lead instruction role in the class and the other or others – students – rotate among the learners, providing support as needed, observing how they work in a group, clearing up doubts or supporting students with difficulties. The role of leading could alter in later moments in such a way that the teacher can work to serve individual students or particular groups (for example, the especially advanced).

- *Parallel co-teaching.* The co-teachers work with different groups of students in different sections of the classroom. Students can frequently be regrouped to benefit from the teaching of the instructors. This form offers many varied situations. Divide the class up to monitor comprehension; create centres of interest; offer explanations in rotating groups; use different learning spaces (outside and inside the school); support different styles or learning preferences (featuring a visual explanation in one group, a kinaesthetic approach elsewhere, etc.); or provide supplemental instruction (giving more help or generating challenges for deeper learning).
- *Complementary co-teaching.* One co-teacher complements or adds value to the instruction provided by the other. This allows part of the explanation to be contributed regarding varying shape, facilitating understanding, modelling the explanation or supporting it with graphic resources.
- *Team teaching.* This way requires maximum coordination and that the *co-teachers* share responsibility for all the instructional activities (planning, acting in the classroom and assessing), both assuming responsibility for the learning of all students in the class.

Obviously, as well as co-teaching among teachers, co-teaching with students so that they have the opportunity to learn by teaching requires careful planning. Teachers must be prepared very well regarding the selection and the form of participation of students, the training they receive (to ensure that it is a learning experience for themselves, as they learn to teach) and the monitoring of student *co-teachers* and their evaluation as activities of learning for themselves. The contents of training on teaching which the co-teachers receive in one of these schools include the concept of inclusion, effective instruction, checking understanding, learning styles, multiple intelligences, learning technologies and so on. In fact, students develop the competence of teaching.

This is certainly an interesting way to promote learning through teaching others, allowing schools to be understood as learning communities, where everyone learns and teaches, set up like institutions that themselves learn.

Chapter 6

Teaching others and learning oneself
How can teachers learn by teaching?

Teachers who teach recognize that they learn by teaching. They not only learn didactic aspects, but they redefine and advance in their understanding of the discipline in which they are experts.

Elena Martín (2009: p204)

After seeing in the previous chapters that the activity of teaching – an exclusively human ability – may have a high potential for learning for those who develop it, it seems appropriate to consider that professionals of teaching (teachers, professors, etc.) should know what conditions can help themselves also learn by teaching their students.

It would be paradoxical to want to turn classrooms into communities of learners, but to do so in such a way that the only person who did not learn in classrooms was the teacher. Probably, the teaching profession is one of those that require a more permanent upgrade in light of the demands of the knowledge society. Teachers must be up to date in their area of expertise and how to teach it to help their students to learn. Thus, it is necessary to reconfigure teaching action by seizing the opportunities of learning by teaching, so the actions of the teacher also result in learning opportunities for him- or herself.

Learning by teaching would, in the words of the educational psychologist Elena Martín, give teachers a broader vision of the benefits of education. This would not only be useful for their students, but also for teachers and for society, to the extent that new knowledge is generated. Teachers would become professionals who learn in their daily practice and thus contribute to the establishment of educational institutions where everyone – not only students – learns (Bolívar, 2000). This chapter will review the research evidence on learning by teaching, in order to highlight some principles that derive from it that can help teachers to learn by teaching.

These principles do not replace teaching practices developed by teachers, or the valuable contributions on teaching that the various sciences of education have contributed. Of course, the purpose is much more modest: we try to outline principles – already done by good teachers – to complete teaching activities. In addition, we are convinced that teachers will recognize practices in these principles or examples in their respective contexts or areas of knowledge.

First, we will refer to the predisposition to learn by teaching; and then we will use the classic distinction between pre-activities (before class), inter-activities (in the classroom) and post-activities (after class) (Reynolds, 1989) to highlight actions that can help teachers to learn by teaching.

Predisposition to learning by teaching: my students are a source for my learning

It is clear, and our teaching experience supports it, that if someone does not want to learn something, he or she does not. Learning requires the active participation of the learner and is therefore mediated by will and motivation – motivation that is conveyed through goals or objectives and the expectations of achieving (Alonso Tapia, 2005). If teachers want to learn through the activity of teaching, we must include this objective in our actions and have high expectations for it. So it seems necessary to include that possibility in our notion of teaching and learning, and to deliberately deploy procedures and attitudes that help its achievement. Both issues are the purpose of this section.

In the ZPD, the teacher is also involved

In previous chapters we highlighted that it is understood that the role of the teacher is to provide educational assistance within the Zone of Proximal Development (ZPD) (Vygotsky, 1978), which is defined as the area between what you already know and what you can learn with the help of a mediator (the person who mediates between the mental activity of the apprentice and the source of the new information, in this case the teacher). Therefore, the role of the teacher is to know what the students know, their previous knowledge or *level of actual development* (LAD), and what they can get to know with the help of others – their level of potential development (LPD) – by managing scaffolding and support within the ZPD, which will progressively be withdrawn as students increase their LAD.

In classrooms, this explanation of learning and the facilitator role of the teacher require the development of adapted assistance, responding to these zones of development, and therefore begins with the initial assessment of the students. Asking them, watching them – in short, approaching them, to accompany them in their learning process. But we must also remember that the ZPD is not a halo that surrounds our students, nor a static space that emerges after the initial assessment of their knowledge or what they propose to learn. The ZPD emerges from joint activity and all participants, not just the apprentice, can learn (Wells, 1999). Which means that in offering contingent help, teachers have opportunities to reflect deeply on what they teach. In the words of teachers Barbara Galbraith and Mary Van Tassell: "As teachers, we can help learners by the questions we ask and guidance we give. But we can ourselves also receive help and guidance from the questions and suggestions of learners if only we are ready to accept them" (quoted in Wells, 1999: p312).

So, if we are predisposed, we can ourselves learn from the interactions that occur when, as experts, we help our students. And if we go beyond, and from the questions and interests of our students we gear ourselves towards learning objectives of which we do not know enough or that constitute social knowledge that is still in construction (something increasingly common), our own teacher training opportunities will multiply exponentially. In this type of expansive learning (Engeström, 1987), with collective zones of proximal development, the roles of teachers and learners become blurred and all participants – including the teacher – learn in the process.

An extreme example of this is found in an initiative of the Mobile World Centre of Barcelona, an innovative experience in which thousands of secondary students are developing apps for mobile devices through an optional subject. Situated in an R&D context, the teachers of the subject, supported by external experts, assume teaching objectives linked to the interests of the student – in the creation and development of a particular application – which, without a doubt, offers opportunities for them to learn along with their students.

Sharing the learning process with our students

Unlike transmissive forms of teaching, where teachers stand in front of their students and lecture or transfer information, forms which can promote learning by teaching place teachers side by side with their students, accompanying them and sharing learning opportunities with them. In this way, teachers not only contribute to pedagogical support, but also they become a model of the apprentice.

For this it is necessary that we have procedures and attitudes which take precedence over our teaching role, and which must be explained and negotiated with our students, because some of these collide directly with the traditional concept of teacher, dominant in the culture of the transmission. In brief:

- *Our capabilities are also in development.* We are not professionals with finished knowledge: we need to develop our capabilities, insofar as knowledge of our field of education (which is always being updated and that always supports deeper and more extended knowledge forms) is related to the teaching of content-related knowledge.
- *We are also learning with our students.* The processes of teaching and learning that we promote in our classrooms, with our students, must be rich and varied to allow for the possibility that we will learn ourselves, as privileged guests of the process. If we use the well-known analogy of learning as an organized tour, where the teacher is the guide, we should make sure to include in the route some destinations or visits that are unknown to us.
- *We accept what we do not know and turn it into learning objectives.* We must rid ourselves of the old pressure to appear before our students as someone who knows everything, but rather to show we are someone who helps them to learn and who learns with them. Which means recognizing what we do not know – for example, in response to a student question – and celebrating it as a learning opportunity for everyone, including the teacher. In the knowledge society, it is wanting to keep an omniscient identity which can lead us to lose prestige, when our students can check, often very quickly through the Internet, the answers that

we offer. The recognition of error and ignorance is the starting point of learning – also for the teachers.

- *We seek support for the learning of our students and for our own learning.* Recognizing that we do not have a monopoly on knowledge nor on teaching entails resorting systematically to other sources of support for learning – both for students and ourselves – in the environment: other teachers, families of elementary school students, experts from the community, students of advanced courses, or, through technology, people or resources from other countries.

We have briefly seen some considerations that may predispose us to learning by teaching our students. Let us now consider lines of action that can help us to include this principle throughout the three phases of our teaching performance – not necessarily linear, but rather recursive.

Pre-active: learning when preparing classes for learning

The evidence in Chapter 3 showed us that learning to teach others has a higher learning potential than learning only for ourselves. Reviewing the materials, identifying our own gaps, organizing and reformulating the contents, identifying what is basic (distinguishing it from secondary) to present information with sense, turning it into knowledge – all of these are activities which may explain the learning potential in preparing to teach others. If, in addition, we use forms of co-teaching, we prepare the classes in collaboration with other teachers, our opportunities to learn in this pre-active phase will undoubtedly be much greater (Duran & Miquel, 2003). Since this activity is part of the daily work of teachers, let us look at some considerations that can help us to convert these spaces into fertile times for our own learning. As we assume that teachers already prepare classes on a regular basis, we will only highlight additional actions in this pre-active work.

Using the positive stress of audience

Beyond professional responsibility, one thing that helps teachers to prepare explanations is the desire to avoid embarrassment in front of the students (such as being asked about something that we don't know). We should change that kind of stress for another that can also give positive pressure, motivating us to prepare classes well. If we think that our students should share the organization of the contents (understanding what we explain) and have the maximum opportunities to learn as much as possible, this will constitute sufficient pressure to feel stimulated to thoroughly prepare classes. As in other social activities, excessive anxiety has negative consequences, but a certain degree of positive stress with regard to our audiences – our students – can act as an element of motivation.

Adjust explanations and objectives to prior knowledge

Recognizing the importance of providing educational help within the ZPD, something beyond what our students already know, it is crucial to make an initial assessment before undertaking a learning unit. A learning unit is understood as a work proposal of limited duration, which organizes a set of teaching and learning activities that respond with specificity to the elements of curriculum: objectives and contents, methodology, timing and evaluation. Learning units (also called themes, lessons) can take the form of projects or combine various methodologies.

The results of this initial assessment should give us clues to adjust the contents and activities planned to develop our students' prior knowledge. This setting or reprocessing of the unit can lead to the need to add new concepts, present the information with other sequences or replace activities with others. All these settings will allow us to get deeper into the materials we use to teach.

Likewise, the initial assessment is an excellent instrument for collecting student interests regarding the learning objective that we propose. Choose assessments and turn them into learning objectives. This will not only improve the motivation of the students, but also develop our own opportunities to learn. This is true especially when we use methodologies such as group investigation or projects, which allow students to reach the learning objective through contents or methods that they themselves choose. Finally, more complex concerns or curiosities, even far away from the learning objective proposed, can be used to design activities for deepening or enlargement that are also clearly positioned within the zone of development of the teacher.

Prepare the explanations in various formats

It is obvious that our students have different learning styles or preferences. Some of them prefer to receive information aurally (to listen to), others visually (to read or see), and others through movement (to do). Also we know that there are, as Howard Gardner (1999) showed, many different intelligences: musical, visual, verbal, logical, mathematical, kinaesthetical, interpersonal, intrapersonal and naturalistic. Each student may better understand the contents if they are presented in a certain way: narrative, numerical, logical, existential, aesthetic, practical or interpersonal.

In the same vein, the Universal Design for Learning (CAST, 2008) is a proposal for building inclusive classrooms where all students have maximum opportunities to learn. This suggests the use of multiple means of representation to give learners various ways of acquiring information and knowledge. This includes providing options for facilitating perception (customizing the display of information and searching for alternatives to auditory and visual information); a variety of language and symbols to enhance access (defining vocabulary and symbols, or illustrating the key concepts non-linguistically); and comprehension (activating background knowledge, highlighting critical issues and their relationships to ensure their processing and future transfer). The simple challenge that can create the presentation of a basic concept in another representational format (through a drawing or sound) can offer us a good learning opportunity.

Contextualize the explanation, activities and examples

We should use the knowledge that we have about our students and their environment, which allows us to contextualize our explanations, adjusting them to their realities and interests. The search for examples, illustrations and, above all, respondents' realities will increase the functionality and usefulness of learning, and its authenticity – influencing the construction of the sense of what students learn. But, from the teacher's point of view, it will allow us to win a depth of applied knowledge of what we intend to teach.

Sometimes, adjusting the activities and content to student needs and contexts can be an easy task, and it will be enough if we are just interested in the social environment in which they live. But on other occasions, when we work, for instance, with students of different cultural backgrounds, it is more complex. In these cases, we can use the students themselves so that they take ownership of the information and transfer it into their respective contexts, themselves proposing some activities or problems. The transfer of issues we intend to teach to these new contexts, little known for us, will provide us with rich learning opportunities.

Interactive: promoting bidirectionality to learn as we teach

Interactive teaching, relating to the work we do in contact with our students in the classroom, could offer even greater opportunities for learning, if that interaction moves away from one-way or transmissive formats and recognizes the student as a resource for teacher learning (Cortese, 2005). Therefore, in this section we will focus exclusively on formats that deliberately promote the active participation of the students, with the aim of bringing us to the context of bidirectionality.

Build knowledge reflectively

If the preparation of the explanation (and its subsequent performance) allowed us to *learn to teach*, the classroom interaction is when we can assess – from student participation – our own knowledge and understanding, if the explanations make sense and are logical. It is, in the terms of Roscoe and Chi (2007), going beyond *saying* knowledge (summarizing information, describing procedures or constructing responses), which at best can help us to strengthen the memory and may be a source of learning only in the first few times we teach something.

Instead of *saying knowledge*, higher learning opportunities come from *reflective knowledge building*, implying that learners have an active role in this process, which will be characterized by participation in a dialogue, where our educational help is offered through intertwined communicative exchanges. Through this educational dialogue, we will have the opportunity to develop the metacognitive activity which can help us to learn ourselves: knowing from our students (their faces, questions, contributions and silences) our own degree of knowledge about what we teach and the quality of the pedagogical support that we offer.

Asking deep questions

To enhance the active participation of the students, first we should ask questions. Questions form part of the classical structure of tripartite dialogue in the classroom,

Initiation-Response-Feedback or IRF (Sinclair & Coulthard, 1975), in which the teacher launches a discursive episode which leads to asking for student answers. Many times teachers ask simple questions about the presented contents, seeming to want literal or superficial understanding of what they have just explained. In fact, the teacher already knows the answer before posing the question.

Without downplaying such kind of questions, they do not offer us opportunities to learn ourselves, compared to those which, far away from *saying* knowledge, require an effort on our part to gain in depth of understanding. We can call them deep questions or *thought-provoking questions* (King, 2008). It is asking questions which relate the prior knowledge of our students with new knowledge; that will help them reorganize their mental models or their previous conceptions; and that will oblige them to keep generating inferences (going beyond what they already know or material which we present them), reflecting on what they knew or they must learn (in the form of metacognitive monitoring).

Such questions induce high-level cognitive processes, for whoever raises them – in this case, the teacher – and for whoever answers them. The effort to build them (deliberately causing students to think in depth, contrasting concepts, applying them, finding causal relationships) offers us a valuable opportunity to learn ourselves. We have to formulate these processes and at the same time reflect on ideas, principles and relations to recombine in order to respond. All this allows us to reorganize and deepen our own understanding and, at the same time, identify our own knowledge gaps (King, 1998).

Answering deep questions

Questioning involves asking and answering. If asking deep questions can offer us opportunities to learn by teaching, answering student questions (if they have those characteristics) may also do so. We don't want to say that we should not promote or answer literal or superficial questions. But if we want to have opportunities to learn, we must deliberately encourage students to ask questions in depth.

In the same way that when we present this kind of question we need time and resources to prepare them, our students will need time too. Some of those questions may arise spontaneously, and so it will be very necessary to create a social atmosphere that encourages questions and to recognize the importance of these contributions. But in other cases, it might not be enough to make students feel comfortable, and we will need to provide guides and reflection times to create and formulate this social space. Thus, for example, after a class, we can offer a thought guideline sheet (Monereo, Pozo & Castelló, 2001) that helps us to formulate deep questions on the contents to be presented at the next session.

The answer to these questions will allow us, to a greater or lesser degree, to step outside our comfort zone and feel challenges that can lead us into learning sexperiences. In some cases – in the best of cases, from a point of view of learning interest – we will have no answer to a question. We may find ourselves with unexpected questions that are related to the objective and that we had not previously contemplated.

The reflection that the teacher should make before the relevant, but unexpected, student question is a powerful source of learning for the teachers themselves (Leikin & Zazkis, 2010).

In the presence of one of these questions we have at least three possibilities: (1) to turn the question into a target of our learning, and answer it later; (2) to make it an aim of extension for the students who are interested (collecting, for example, its results in a portfolio or presenting these results to the rest of the class); or (3) to consider the question as a target for the class, and include it in the learning unit, answering it as a group through activities we co-propose.

While the emergence of questions and interests by students may be the basis for the use of learning methods based on projects or group investigation, it could also be the basis for the elaboration of problematic situations, for example, in the University of Problem-Based Learning (PBL) (Araujo & Sastre, 2008). Giving priority to the interest and the contextualization of these problems is the goal of authentic PBL (Barrows & Wee Keng Neo, 2007). In all cases, the identity of the teacher should not be threatened if we propose to our students that this type of activity is occurring because we have agreed that the class is a learning community, where all – teacher included – learn from the challenges we set ourselves.

We also know that when teachers show that they also learn from the contributions of the students, student motivation is improved. Jesús Alonso Tapia (1998, 2005), offering principles for the organization of motivational instruction, describes a number of elements to arouse and sustain the interest of students. In addition to activating curiosity, showing relevance, organizing the work in teams and offering opportunities to decide, he insists on explicitly promoting the modifiable character of intelligence and capability, helping students to become aware of their learning. But at the same time, he includes the need that teachers model themselves on this principle, realizing that they also learn in the process of teaching.

Listening and observing actively

Active listening to the contributions of our students, linked to questioning in depth, is an essential procedure to create bidirectional reflective knowledge building contexts, offering us opportunities to learn by teaching. Listening and actively observing our students, not only when they interact with us but also when they interact with their peers in the formats of cooperation that we can promote in the classroom, allows us to discover how students think and how to deal with learning tasks. Learning about them, the decisions they take in the resolution of the problem process and the difficulties they have and their ways of overcoming them allows us to build practical knowledge of great value for the adjustment of the pedagogical support that we provide.

Opportunities to learn by observing others, in this case how our students work, can be increased when students deploy experimental procedures that test alternative or innovative methods, simply not foreseen by us, which will lead to reflection on such problematic situations. The modelling of thinking is the effort made by the teacher, as an expert in a subject, to explain what he or she is thinking when solving a particular problem or when learning a specific content. Generally, teachers, in front of their students, resolve the problem by thinking aloud. It is a way of making transparent to the students something that is normally hidden: the process that underlies the accomplishment of tasks (Monereo, Pozo & Castelló, 2001). In addition, the observation of ourselves when modelling such procedures allows us to be aware of the activities involved in tasks and to reflect out loud, to the audience of our students, the necessary decisions on the processes that we are teaching. Both thinking aloud and observing ourselves can create learning by teaching.

Promoting cooperation among students

The systematic use of cooperative learning in the classroom, through techniques or methods such as those included in the previous chapter, is a key element to promote the context of bidirectionality. Peer interaction and mutual help potentially increase the opportunities to learn by teaching, also for the teacher. First, when students work cooperatively, the pattern of interaction in tripartite IRF becomes more complex, replacing teacher feedback with peer collaborative dialogue (Duran & Monereo, 2005) or adding collaboration and evaluation to such a sequence (Graesser, Bowers, Hacker & Person, 1997). The possibilities of peer interaction are enriched, and the classroom is filled with multidirectional interactions that turn it into a community, where members are learning from each other.

From the sociocultural perspective it is the team – and not only its members – who create unity of processing and social knowledge building (Kumpulainen & Wray, 2002). Learning tasks are not resolved only with the mental activity of each teammate, but by teamwork. This makes it easier for teachers to meet and adjust their help and support to these broader thinking units. If instead of 50 students working individually, we attend to 10 teams of 5 students, the opportunities to offer immediate assistance – as soon as the students ask for it – and adjust the pedagogical help are obviously much higher. And this last aspect is the most important, because it allows us to move from *saying* knowledge to the building of reflection.

Instead of giving the correct answer to the question, we have the context to answer with another question or hints (scaffolding supports) located in the zone of development, to encourage the team to make the mental activity – the effort – to resolve the issue, and accordingly to ensure its learning. But this scaffolding feedback from teachers requires greater activity on their part, which gives more opportunities to learn by teaching.

When we have the class working in teams, observation and continuous assessment possibilities grow dramatically. The teacher role is transformed, giving time to carefully observe the process of student work, which allows using observation records to collect data for ongoing assessment (Gillies, 2007). If we have already mentioned the potential of learning from observation of an activity, the learning process assessment is undoubtedly a source which allows us to indirectly assess the quality of our teaching help. From difficulties and mechanisms of overcoming them observed in the teams, we will learn which specific elements we need to improve in our teaching performance.

Finally, as discussed when cooperative learning methods were presented, teamwork allows different activities to be easily presented in the classroom in parallel (teams working for the same learning objective, but through different contents, or teams working at different levels of the same objective), allowing for any team to reach levels of deepening thought that bring learning to the teacher.

Sharing teaching with others

As we have argued previously, the use of cooperative learning in the classroom requires that we share the ability to teach with our students. It involves organizing the peer interactions so that there are systematic episodes in which students teach –and learn by teaching. But there are methods such as group investigation (Sharan & Sharan, 1994), explained in the previous chapter, in which students present their results to the whole of the class, offering learning opportunities for everyone, including the teacher.

But beyond students, a great way to share teaching is the presence of two teachers in the classroom, in *co-teaching* (Lorenz, 1998). The joint work of two teachers, with all its varieties (Villa, Thousand & Nevin, 2010), and with varying degrees of teacher support, not only allows students to receive more and better attention (basic for inclusive education, Huguet, 2009), but also allows teachers to learn from one another (Miquel, 2006). The presence of a colleague in the class increases the chances of reflection on teaching – both in the situation of the classroom and in the post-class, as we will mention later. Co-teaching also provides a sense of accompaniment and support needed to incorporate innovations in our classrooms and, therefore, increase the possibilities for training and professional development (Rytivaara & Kershner, 2012).

The presence of other people who teach in our classes can be extended, as in many schools, by inviting student family members – experts in certain subjects, often through their work experience – to share knowledge with the students, and with the teacher. There are many studies that show conclusively the positive effects of family participation, both in student academic performance and in quality of education improvement (OFSTED, 2001). In this last aspect, the presence of experienced parents who support learning also provides learning potential for the teachers themselves.

Finally, we may share our teaching activity with people in the community that provide knowledge, in the form of professional or specific skills. Thus, for example, the *Index for Inclusion* (Booth & Ainscow, 2002), a guide to help schools to respond to the educational needs of all students without exception, urges schools to use all the resources available in the school environment educationally. To do this, it suggests using a long list that includes nongovernmental organizations, businesses, leaders of ethnic minorities, associations of volunteers, retired people and so on. The only thing that is required to deploy and use the vast resources available in communities is a creative imagination and time to organize it all (Longworth, 2003). And all this is enhanced by the opportunities that Internet offers, to connect our classroom with people and institutions from all over the world. Taking advantage of these resources will provide us with real chances of learning by teaching.

Evaluation as a mechanism to assess our performance

We have talked about the importance of initial assessment to explore the development of our students and to use their knowledge to adjust our actions and build a bidirectional context characterized by reflective knowledge building. It is obvious that, in addition to this, evaluation takes two large and equally necessary forms (Stake, 2004): the formative, referring to assessment in the process of working which gives feedback to enhance that working, and the summative, providing a statement on the level of final attainment of the objective when it is too late to do anything about it. However, for the purposes of this section we will focus on the formative evaluation, because, as suggested by Álvarez (2012), it is the key form of educational evaluation.

Through formative evaluation, we know why our students are learning: how they construct and organize knowledge, solve difficulties and overcome problems with mechanisms and procedures. This will allow us, as teachers, to develop professional knowledge to learn how to adjust and improve the quality of our teaching. Formative evaluation, which implies offering feedback for the improvement of learning processes, helps the student to learn better, but at the same time helps the teacher to teach better. As Álvarez stated, when teachers confirm that a student or group are not learning, they must discover the causes that provoke such an unwanted situation. Evaluation, especially the formative, is a source of learning for teachers to correct their pedagogical support and teaching performance, by adjusting and improving.

Post-active: shared and reflective learning spaces for learning with others

As we have seen, teachers can learn by preparing and giving classes. But when we leave the classroom, the opportunities to learn by teaching continue. In the post-active phase, teachers can also reflect on what allowed us to learn and what we have done (or what we have left undone). A personal reflection in the form of a retrospective analysis (Lampert, 2001) can help us to continue learning, thanks to our teaching. Even so, as we are committed to a social vision of learning, in this last section we focus on the building of social spaces to share and reflect with others on our teaching practices (Perrenoud, 2004).

Having discussion and reflection spaces, based on the analysis of our own educational innovation, combined with contrasting or comparing with other professional perspectives, allows the provision of peer interaction – in this case between teachers – concerning characteristics that promote conceptual change (Martín & Cervi, 2006). This interaction can take multiple forms, depending on the characteristics of the participants: mentoring with teachers-in-training, collaboration between colleagues or network support and so on. In short, it is characterized by collaboration and reflection spaces (Schön, 1991), where teachers can build and rebuild from the riches of what already exists, learning to reflect on what guides decisions in practice (thoughts, feelings, expectations and beliefs), to create actions that substantially improve what happens in classrooms by being in tune with the current educational needs of society.

These approximations converge in a series of shared principles that shape new models of teacher training as environments that are based on concrete classroom practice using peer shared reflection about conceptions and actions, promoting an active professional development with impact on teaching quality (Ruiz-Bikandi & Camps, 2007).

Using colleague teacher observation

The presence of a teacher in our classroom, whether as a teacher support, as a practitioner or in other forms of co-teaching, can be exploited to collect data that will allow further reflection on how to improve our teaching (Rhodes, Sokes & Hampton, 2004). Observation among teachers requires prior agreement on what will be observed in particular and how they will do it.

The objectives of the observation can be very different, since the focus might be the introduction of an innovation or the delimitation of a problem to find a solution together. Observation can be done on using a schedule or register, in an eco-friendly format, which can lead the observer to participate by performing the role of support teacher. Alternatively, using video (Brophy, 2003) allows teachers not only the possibility of viewing the same episode several times, but also of observing themselves. The way that observation feedback is offered, from the observation register or from data obtained by the analysis of the video – which can be accompanied by small clips – also must be agreed upon and, in any case, should not take the form of an evaluation or judgment, but of an opportunity to learn and improve teaching performance (Ewans, 2001).

Using data to improve teaching

As teachers, we can learn from the analysis of our teaching practice by using other data to reflect on peer learning (between teachers). The elements that can serve such reflection come from different sources (Santos Guerra, 2001):

- *Content contributed by experts or discussions of articles.* The school library will have books and journals about education and teaching, whether on paper or online.
- *Results of external evaluations or evidence of achievement of educational skills.* These results should serve as diagnostics to help design actions to improve things, rather than to classify teachers or schools.
- *Input from external consultants or critical friends* who value concrete practices. Training in schools should adopt a constructivist perspective, on the basis

of the analysis of the practice of the classroom and providing resources for improvement.

- *Assessments of students, former students or families* (in the case of basic education). The voice of the students should be considered a source for improvement and for teacher professional development.
- *Exchange of good practices from other schools*. The creation of networks of schools for exchanging experiences – learning from each other – and generating spaces in which teachers themselves as creators of knowledge experience, evaluate and disseminate innovative experiences that can promote substantial changes.

In all these cases, there is a certain conflict between current educational practices – supported by data or observations – and theoretical concepts. They raise different perspectives that need to be translated into plans or actions to improve teacher performance. Knowing the need for the improvement of teacher practices, it is necessary to start a process of accompaniment – to which a shared reflection space is essential – in order to incorporate improvement in the teaching repertoire. In many cases, when concerning methodological changes, it is necessary that these changes sustain over time and are incorporated into educational school projects, which require leadership to change (Hargreaves & Fink, 2006).

Perhaps it could go without saying that what we have here located in the post-active phase is the generation of changes or plans for the improvement of teaching practice situated at the beginning of the cycle, offering the teacher opportunities to continue learning by preparing the unit and the class. Without a doubt, professional teachers have many opportunities to teach by learning and learn by teaching themselves. It depends on us taking advantage of it to be involved in continuous updating and learning, which will help us to build the teacher role in the knowledge society. But, above all, it will enable us to enjoy our profession in a more satisfactory and happy way.

References

Acaso, M. (2013). *Reduvolution. Hacer la revolución en la educación*. Barcelona: Paidós.

Adell, J. & Castañeda, L. (2010). Los Entornos Personales de Aprendizaje (PLEs): Una nueva manera de entender el aprendizaje. In M. Roig & A. R. Fiorucci (Eds.). *Claves para la investigación en innovación y calidad educativas*. Alcoy: Marfil.

Algás, P., Ballester, J., Carbonell, L. Diez, M. C. et al. (2010). *Los proyectos de trabajo en el aula*. Barcelona: Graó.

Allen, V. (1976). *Children as teachers: Theory and research on tutoring*. New York: Academic Press.

Alonso Tapia, J. (2005). *Motivar en la escuela, motivar en la familia*. Madrid: Morata.

Alonso Tapia, J. (1998). *Motivación y aprendizaje en el aula*. Madrid: Santillana.

Álvarez, F., Rodríguez-Perez, J. R., Sanz-Ablanedo, E. & Fernández-Martínez, M. (2008). Aprender enseñando: Elaboración de materiales didácticos que facilitan el aprendizaje autónomo. *Formación Universitaria*, *1*(6), 19–28.

Álvarez, J. M. (2012). Pensar la evaluación como recurso de aprendizaje. In B. Jarauta & F. Imbernón (Eds.). *Pensando en el futuro de la educación. Una nueva escuela para el siglo XXII* (139–158). Barcelona: Graó.

Álvarez, P. & González, M. (2007). El asesoramiento y la tutoría de carrera en la Enseñanza Superior: Resultados de un programa de atención al alumnado en la universidad de La Laguna. *Revista de Educación*, *9*, 95–110.

Anderberg, E., Axelsson, A., Bengtsson, S., Håkansson, M. & Lindberg, L. (2013). Exploring the use of a teachable agent in a mathematical computer game for preschoolers. In C. Balkenius, A. Gulz, M. Haake & B. Johansson (Eds.). *Intelligent, socially oriented technology* (pp. 161–171). Lund University Cognitive Studies, 154.

Annis, L. F. (1983). The processes and effects of peer tutoring. *Human Learning*, *2*, 39–47.

Araujo, U.F. & Sastre, G. (2008). *El aprendizaje basado en problemas. Una nueva perspectiva de la enseñanza en la Universidad*. Barcelona: Gedisa.

Aronson, E. & Patnoe, S. (2011). *Cooperation in the classroom: The Jigsaw method*. New York: Pinter & Martin Ltd.

Azmitia, M. & Hesser, J. (1993). Why siblings are important agents of cognitive development: A comparison of siblings and peers. *Child Development*, *64*, 430–444.

Bargh, J. & Schul, Y. (1980). On the cognitive benefits of teaching. *Journal of Educational Psychology*, *75*(2), 593–604.

Baron-Cohen, S., Leslie, A. & Frith, U. (1985). Does the autistic child have 'theory of mind'? *Cognition*, *21*, 37–46.

Barrows, H. S. & Wee Keng Neo, L. (2007). *Principles and practice of PBL*. Singapore: Pearson.

Baudrit, A. (2012). *Relations d'aide entre élèves à l'école*. Bruselas: De Boeck.

Bauman, Z. (2000). *Liquid modernity*. Cambridge: Polity.

Benware, C. A. & Deci, E. L. (1984). Quality of learning with an active versus passive motivational set. *American Educational Research Journal, 21,* 755–765.

Biswas, G. Schwartz, D. Leelawong, K. & Vye, N. (2005). Learning by teaching: A new agent paradigm for educational software. *Applied Artificial Intelligence, 19,* 363–392.

Blanch, S., Duran, D., Valdebenito, V. & Flores, M. (2013). The effects and characteristics of family involvement on a peer tutoring programme to improve the reading comprehension competence. *European Journal of Psychology Education, 28*(1), 101–119.

Blunt, R. (2003). *Communities at the speed of business.* New York: Universe, Inc.

Bolívar, A. (2000). *Los centros educativos como organizaciones que aprenden.* Madrid: Muralla.

Booth, T. & Ainscow, M. (2002). *Index for inclusion.* Bristol: CSIE.

Boud, D., Cohen, R. & Sampson, J. (2001). *Peer learning in higher education.* London: Kogan Page.

Boud, D. & Molloy, E. (Eds.) (2013). *Feedback in higher and professional education: Understanding it and doing it well.* New York: Routledge.

Brandenburger, A. & Nalebuff, B. (1998). *Co-opetition.* New York: Currecy Doubleday.

Brophy, J. (Ed.) (2003). *Using video in teacher education.* Elmont, NY: Elsevier.

Buhrmester, D. & Furman, W. (1990). Perceptions of sibling relationships during middle childhood and adolescence. *Child Development, 61,* 1387–1398.

Burns, E. (2006). Pause, prompt and praise: Peer tutored reading for pupils with learning difficulties. *British Journal of Special Education, 33*(2), 62–67.

Carr, N. (2010). *The shallows: What the Internet is doing to our brains.* New York: W.W. Norton.

Cassany, D. (1993). *Reparar l'escriptura. Didàctica de la correcció de l'escrit.* Graó: Barcelona.

CAST (2008). *Universal design for learning guidelines version 1.0.* Wakefield, MA: Author.

Castañeda, L. & Adell, J. (Eds.). (2013). *Entornos personales de aprendizaje: Claves para el ecosistema educativo en red.* Alcoy: Marfil.

Chancel, G., Jordana, M. & Pericon, R. (2008). *La tutoría entre iguales en el marco del EEES: Cinco años de funcionamiento del Programa de Asesores de Estudiantes en la UAB.* Barcelona: UAB.

Chase, C. C., Chin, D. B., Oppezzo, M. A. & Schwartz, D. L. (2009). Teachable agents and the protégé effect: Increasing the effort towards learning. *Journal of Science Education and Technology, 18*(4), 334–352.

Chi, M. T. H., Bassok, M., Lewis, M. W., Reimann, P. & Glaser, R. (1989). Self-explanations: How students study and use examples in learning to solve problems. *Cognitive Science, 13,* 145–182.

Cloward, R. D. (1967). Studies in tutoring. *Journal of Experimental Education, 36,* 14–25.

Cobo, C. & Moravec, J. W. (2011). *Aprendizaje invisible. Hacia una nueva ecología de la educación.* Barcelona: Publicacions i Edicions de la Universitat de Barcelona.

Cohen, P., Kulik, J. & Kulik, C. (1982). Educational outcomes of tutoring: A meta-analysis of findings. *American Educational Research Journal, 19*(2), 237–248.

Coll, C. & Monereo, C. (2008). *Psicología de la Educación Virtual.* Madrid: Morata.

Colomina, R. & Onrubia, J. (2001). Interacción educativa y aprendizaje escolar: la interacción entre alumnos. In C. Coll, J. Palacios & A. Marchesi (Eds.). *Desarrollo psicológico y educación II. Psicología de la educación escolar* (pp. 415–437). Alianza: Madrid.

Cortese, C. (2005). Learning through teaching. *Management Learning, 36*(1), 87–115.

Cross, J. (2006). *Informal learning: Rediscovering the natural pathways that inspire innovation and performance.* San Francisco, CA: John Wiley & Sons.

Crouch, C. & Mazur, E. (2001). Peer Instruction: Ten years of experience and results. *American Association of Physics Teachers, 69*(9), 970–977.

Dale, E. (1946). *Audio-visual methods in teaching.* New York: The Dryden Press.

Damon, W. & Phelps, E. (1989). Critical distinctions among three approaches to peer education. *International Journal of Educational Research, 13*(1), 9–19.

Daou, M., Lohse, K. R. & Miller, M. W. (2016). Expecting to teach enhances motor learning and information processing during practice. *Human Movement Science, 49*, 336–345.

Dawkins, R. (1976). *The selfish gene*. Oxford: Oxford University Press.

Definition and Selection of Competencies (DeSeCo) (2002). *Key competencies for a successful life and a well-functioning society*. Paris: OECD.

Dentler, D. (1994). Cooperative learning and American history. *Cooperative Learning and College Teaching, 4*(3), 9–12.

Departament d'Educació (2007). *Decret 142/2007, de 26 de juny, pel qual s'estableix l'ordenació dels ensenyaments de l'educació primària*. DOGC, 4915.

Departament d'Ensenyament (2010). *Document per a l'organització i funcionament dels centres públics d'educació secundària*. Barcelona: Generalitat de Catalunya.

Dewey, J. (1916). *Democracy and education: An introduction to the philosophy of education*. New York: Macmillan.

Díaz-Aguado, M. J. (2005). *Aprendizaje cooperativo. Hacia una nueva síntesis entre la eficacia docente y la educación en valores*. Madrid: Santillana.

Dillenbourg, P. (Ed.) (1999). *Collaborative learning: Cognitive and computational approaches*. Oxford: Elsevier Science Ltd.

Dilts, R. (2003). *Coaching. Herramientas para el cambio*. Barcelona: Urano.

Duran, D. (2009a). Aprender a cooperar. Del grupo al equipo. In J. I. Pozo & M. del P. Pérez (Eds.). *La Psicología del aprendizaje universitario: La formación en competencias* (pp. 182–195). Madrid: Ediciones Morata.

Duran, D. (2009b). El aprendizaje entre alumnos como apoyo a la inclusión. In C. Giné (Ed.). *La educación inclusiva. De la exclusión a la plena participación de todo el alumnado* (pp. 95–111). Barcelona: Horsori.

Duran, D. (2007). ¿Solos ante el peligro? Las gafas que nos impiden ver la importancia de las interacciones entre alumnos. In M. Castelló (Ed.). *Enseñar a pensar* (pp. 85–113). Madrid: Ministerio de Educación y Ciencia.

Duran, D. (2012). Utilizando el trabajo en equipo. Estructurar la interacción a través de métodos y técnicas. In J. C. Torrego & A. Negro. *Aprendizaje cooperativo en las aulas* (pp. 139–166). Madrid: Alianza.

Duran, D. & Blanch, S. (2007). Una experiència de coavaluació: Situar l'avaluació en el procés d'aprenentatge i afavorir que els estudiants de magisteri aprenguin a avaluar treballs escrits. *IV Jornades de Campus d'Innovació Docent*. Barcelona: UAB.

Duran, D., Blanch, S., Thurston, A. & Topping, K. J. (2010). Tutoría entre iguales recíproca y virtual para la mejora de habilidades lingüísticas en español e inglés. *Infancia y Aprendizaje, 33*(2), 209–222.

Duran, D. & Flores, M. (2015). Prácticas de tutoría entre iguales en universidades del Estado Español y de Iberoamérica. *Revista Iberoamericana sobre Calidad, Eficacia y Cambio en Educación, 13*(1), 5–17.

Duran, D., Flores, M., Oller, M., Thomson-Garay, L. & Vera, I. (2016). *Reading in pairs. Peer tutoring for reading and speaking in English as a foreign language*. Barcelona: Horsori.

Duran, D. & Miquel, E. (2003). Cooperar para enseñar y aprender. *Cuadernos de Pedagogía, 331*, 73–76.

Duran, D. & Monereo, C. (2012). *Entramado. Métodos de aprendizaje cooperativo y colaborativo*. Barcelona: Horsori.

Duran, D. & Monereo, C. (2005). Styles and sequences of cooperative interaction in fixed and reciprocal peer tutoring. *Learning & Instruction, 15*, 179–199.

Duran, D. & Monereo, C. (2008). The impact of peer tutoring on student self-concept, self-esteem and satisfaction. *School Psychology International, 29*, 481–499.

Duran, D. & Vidal, V. (2004). *Tutoría entre iguales. De la teoría a la práctica*. Barcelona: Graó.

Ehly, S., Keith, T. Z. & Bratton, B. (1987). The benefits of tutoring: An exploration of expectancy and outcomes. *Contemporary Educational Psychology, 12*, 131–134.

Einstein, A. (1949). *The world as I see it*. New York: Philosophical Library.

Ellis, S. & Gauvin, M. (1992). Social and cultural influences on children's collaborative interactions. In L. Winegar & J. Valsiner (Eds.). *Children's development within social context* (pp. 155–180). Hillsdale, NJ: Lawrence Erlbaum Associates.

Engeström, Y. (1999). Activity theory and individual and social transformation. In Y. Engeström, R. Miettinen & R. L. Punamäki-Gitai (Eds.). *Perspectives on activity theory* (pp. 19–38). Cambridge: University Press.

Engeström, Y. (1987). *Learning by expanding. An activity-theoretical approach to developmental research*. Helsinki: Orienta Konsultit Oy.

Eraut, M. (2000). Non-formal learning and tacit knowledge in professional work. *British Journal of Educational Psychology, 70*, 113–136.

Ewans, D. (2001). *Observation of teaching and learning in adult education*. London: LSDA.

Eyler, J., Giles, J. & Dwight, E. (1999). *Where's the learning in Service-Learning?* San Francisco, CA: Jossey-Bass.

Falchikov, N. (2001). *Learning together: Peer tutoring in higher education*. London: Routledge Falmer.

Falchikov, N. & Goldfinch, G. (2000). Student peer assessment in higher education: A meta-analysis comparing peer and teacher marks. *Review of Educational Research, 70*(3), 287–322.

Fantuzzo, J. & Ginsburg-Block, M. (1998). Reciprocal peer tutoring: Developing and testing effective peer collaborations for elementary school students. In K. J. Topping & S. Ehly (Eds.). *Peer-assisted learning* (pp. 121–145). Mahwah, NJ: Lawrence Erlbaum Associates.

Feito, R. (2006). *Otra escuela es posible*. Madrid: Siglo XXI.

Fernández, F. D. & Arco, J. L. (2011). Efectos de un programa de acción tutorial entre universitarios. *Infancia y Aprendizaje, 34*(1), 109–122.

Fernández Enguita, M. (2002). Educación y trabajo en la sociedad informacional. In J. Torreblanca (Ed.). *Los fines de la educación: Una reflexión desde la izquierda*. Madrid: Biblioteca Nueva.

Fiorella, L. & Mayer, R. (2013). The relative benefits of learning by teaching expectancy. *Contemporary Educational Psychology, 38*(4), 281–288.

Flores, M. & Duran, D. (2013). Effects of peer tutoring on reading self-concept. *International Journal of Educational Psychology, 2*(3), 297–324.

Flores, M. & Duran D. (2015). Influence of a Catalan peer tutoring programme on reading comprehension and self-concept as a reader. *Journal of Research in Reading, 39*(3), 330–346.

Fraga, G., Caravalho, R. Hirano, E. & Bollela, V. (2012). Basic life support: Medical students learning by teaching. *Medical Education, 46*, 1099–1136.

Freire, P. (1996). *Pedagogía de la autonomía: Saberes necesarios para la práctica educativa*. México: Siglo XXI.

Freire, P. (1984). *Pedagogía del oprimido*. Madrid: Siglo XXI.

García-Lastra, M. (2013). Educar en la sociedad contemporánea. Hacia un nuevo escenario educativo. *Convergencia: Revista de Ciencias Sociales, 62*, 199–220.

Gardner, H. (1999). *Intelligence reframed: Multiple intelligences for the 21st century*. New York: Basic Books.

Gartner, A., Kohler, M. & Riessmann, F. (1971). *Children teach children: Learning by teaching*. New York: Harper and Row.

Gillies, R. M. (2007). *Cooperative learning: Integrating theory and practice*. Thousand Oaks, CA: Sage Publications.

Gimeno Sacristán, J. (2012). ¿Por qué nos importa la educación del futuro? In B. Jaruata & F. Imbernón (Eds.). *Pensando en el futuro de la educación. Una nueva escuela para el siglo XXII* (pp. 9–17). Barcelona: Graó.

Goldschmid, B. & Goldschmid, M. (1976). Peer teaching in higher education: A review. *Higher Education, 5*(1), 9–33.

González, A. (2013). La experiencia de Cataluña 5 años en el programa paciente experto Catalunya®. *Ponencia V Congreso Nacional de Atención Sanitaria al Paciente Crónico [edición online] 2013.* Accessed from http://v.congresocronicos.org/documentos/ponencias/experiencia-catalunya-paciente-experto.pdf.

González, A., Fabrellas, N., Agramunt, M., Rodríguez, E. & Grifell, E. (2008). De paciente pasivo a paciente activo. Programa paciente experto del Institut Català de la Salut. *Revista de Innovación Sanitaria y Atención Integrada, 1*(1).

Good, T. L. & Brophy, J. E. (1997). *Looking in classrooms.* New York: Addison Wesley Longman.

Goodlad, S. & Hirst, B. (1989). *Peer tutoring: A guide to learning by teaching.* London: K. Page.

Graesser, A., Bowers, C., Hacker, D. & Person, N. (1997). An anatomy of naturalistic tutoring. In K. Hogan & M. Pressley (Eds.). *Scaffolding student learning* (pp. 145–184). New York: Brookline Books.

Graesser, A., D'Mello, S. & Cade, W. (2009). Instruction based on tutoring. In R. E. Mayer & P. A. Alexander (Eds.). *Handbook of research on learning and instruction* (pp. 408–426). New York: Routledge.

Graesser, A. & Person, N. (1994). Question asking during tutoring. *American Educational Research Journal, 31*(1), 104–137.

Greenwood, C. R., Carta, J. & Kamps, D. (1990). Teacher-mediated versus peer-mediated instruction: A review of advantages and disadvantages. In H. C. Foot, M. J. Morgan & R. H. Shute (Eds.). *Children helping children.* Chichester: John Wiley and Sons.

Grisham, D. & Molinelli, P. (2001). *Cooperative learning. Professional's guide.* Westminster, CA: Teacher Created Materials, Inc.

Grzega, J. & Schöner, M. (2008). The didactic model LdL (Lerner durch Lehren) as a way of preparing students for communication in a knowledge society. *Journal of Education for Teaching, 34*(3), 167–175.

Guilmette, J. (2007). *The power of peer learning. Networks and development cooperation.* Ottawa: International Development Research Centre.

Hargreaves, A. & Fink, D. (2006). *Sustainable leadership.* San Francisco: Jossey-Bass.

Harris, J. (2006). *Not two alike.* New York: Norton & CIA.

Harris, J. (1999). *The nature assumption.* New York: Free Press.

Highet, G. (1950). *The art of teaching.* New York: Knopf.

Hogan, D. & Tudge, J. (1999). Implications of Vigotsky's theory for peer leaning. In A. O'Donnell & A. King (Eds.). *Cognitive perspectives on peer learning* (pp. 39–67). Mahwah, NJ: Lawrence Erlbaum Associates.

Huguet, T. (2009). El trabajo colaborativo entre el profesorado como estrategia para la inclusión. In C. Giné (Eds.). *La educación inclusiva. De la exclusión a la plena participación de todo el alumnado* (pp. 81–95). Barcelona: Horsori.

Iacoboni, M. (2008). *Mirroring people. The new science of how we connect with others.* New York: Picador.

Ito, M. (2012). Vivir y aprender con los medios: Resumen de las conclusiones del proyecto digital youth. In R. Díaz, J. Freire, B. Lamb, J. Martín et al. (Eds.). *Educación Expandida* (pp. 236–288). Sevilla: Zemos 98.

Ito, M., Lyman, P., Carter, M. & Thorne, B. (2008). *Living and learning with new media: Summary of findings from the Digital Youth Project.* Chicago, IL: MacArthur Foundation.

Jacoby, B. (1996). *Service-learning in higher education: Concepts and practices.* Michigan: Jossey-Bass.

Johnson, D. & Johnson, R. (2008). Social interdependence theory and cooperative learning: The teacher's role. In R. Gillies, A. Ashman & J. Terwel (Eds). *The teacher's role in implementing cooperative learning in the classroom* (pp. 9–37). New York: Springer.

Johnson, D. & Johnson, R. (1994). Structuring academic controversy. In S. Sharan (Ed.). *Handbook of cooperative learning methods* (pp. 51–65). Westport, CT: Praeger Publishers.

Johnson, D. & Johnson, R. (1990). *Cooperation and competition. Theory and research.* Edina, MN: Instruction Books.

Johnson, D., Johnson, R. & Smith, K. (2007). The state of cooperative learning in postsecondary and professional settings. *Educational Psychology Review*, *19*, 15–29.

Jubany, J. (2012). *Connecta't per aprendre. Aprenentatge social i personalitzat.* Barcelona: Rosa Sensat.

Kafai, Y. & Harel, I. (1991). Learning through design and teaching. In I. Harel & S. Papert (Eds.). *Constructionism.* Norwood, NJ: Ablex Publishing Corporation.

Kagan, S. (1992). *Cooperative learning.* San Juan Capistrano, CA: Resources for Teachers, Inc.

Kagan, S. & Kagan, M. (2009). *Kagan cooperative learning.* San Clemente, CA: Kagan Publishing.

Karmiloff-Smith, A. (1992). *Beyond modularity.* Cambridge, MA: Cambridge University.

King, A. (2008). Structuring peer interaction to promote higher-order thinking and complex learning in cooperative groups. In R. Gillies, A. Ashman & J. Terwel (Eds.). *The teacher's role in implementing cooperative learning in the classroom* (pp. 73–91). New York: Springer.

King, A. (1998). Transactive peer tutoring: Distributing cognition and metacognition, *Educational Psychology Review*, *10*(1), 57–74.

Koschmann, T. (1996). *CSCL: Theory and practice of an emerging paradigm* Mahwah, NJ: Lawrence Erlbaum.

Kumpulainen, K. & Wray, D. (2002). *Classroom interaction and social learning. From theory to practice.* New York: Routledge.

Kurzweil, R. (1999). *The age of spiritual machines: When computers exceed human intelligence.* New York: Viking.

Lacasa, P. (1994). *Aprender en la escuela, aprender en la calle.* Madrid: Visor.

Lambiotte, J. G., Dansereau, D. F., O'Donnell, A. M., Young, M. D., Skaggs, L. P. & Hall, R. H. (1987). Manipulating cooperative scripts for teaching and learning. *Journal of Educational Psychology*, *79*(4), 424–430.

Lampert, M. (2001). *Teaching problems and the problems of teaching.* New Haven, CT: Yale University Press.

Lave, J. & Wenger, E. (1991). *Situated learning. Legitimate peripherical participation.* Cambridge: Cambridge University Press.

Leelalawong, K. (2005). *Using the learning-by-teaching paradigm to design intelligent learning environments.* PhD Dissertation. Computer Science, Vanderbilt University.

Leikin, R. & Zazkis, R. (2010). *Learning through teaching mathematics.* New York: Springer.

Lobato, C. (1998). *El trabajo en grupo. Aprendizaje cooperativo en secundaria.* Bilbao: Euskal Herriko Unibertsitatea.

Longworth, N. (2003). *Lifelong learning in action.* London: Kogan Page Limited.

Lorenz, S. (1998). *Effective in class support. The management of support staff in mainstream and special schools.* London: David Fulton.

Lyman, F. (1992). Think-Pair-Share, Thinktrix, Thinklinks, and weird facts: An interactive system for cooperative learning. In N. Davidson & T. Worsham (Eds). *Enhancing thinking through cooperative learning* (pp.169–181). New York: Teachers College Press.

Marín, J., Barlam, R. & Oliveres, C. (2011). *Enseñar en la sociedad del conocimiento. Reflexiones desde el pupitre.* Barcelona: Horsori.

Martín, E. (2009). Profesorado competente para formar alumnado competente: El reto del cambio docente. In J. I. Pozo & M. del Puy Pérez Echeverría (Eds.). *Psicología del aprendizaje universitario: La formación en competencias* (pp. 199–216). Madrid: Morata.

Martín, E. & Cervi, J. (2006). Modelos de formación docente para el cambio de concepciones en los profesores. In J. I. Pozo, N. Scheuer, M. Pérez, M. Mateos, E. Martín & M. de la Cruz (Eds.). *Nuevas formas de pensar la enseñanza y el aprendizaje. Las concepciones de profesores y alumnos* (pp. 419–434). Barcelona: Graó.

Matsuda, N., Yarzebinski, E., Keiser, V., Raizada, R., Cohen, W. W., Stylianides, G. J. & Koedinger, K. R. (2013). Cognitive anatomy of tutor learning: Lessons learned with SimStudent. *Journal of Educational Psychology, 105*(4), 1152.

Mayer, R. E. & Wittrock, M. C. (2006). Problem solving. In P. Alexander, P. Winne & G. Phye (Eds.). *Handbook of educational psychology*. Mahwah, NJ: Erlbaum.

Mayo, A. & Lank, E. (2003). *Las organizaciones que aprenden*. Barcelona: Gestión 2000.

McCarthey, S. J. & McMahon, S. (1992). From convention to invention: Three approaches to peer interactions during writing. In R. Hertz-Lazarowitz & N. Miller (Eds.). *Interaction in cooperative groups* (pp. 17–35). Cambridge: Cambridge University Press.

McKenna, L. & French, J. (2011). A step ahead: Teaching undergraduate students to be peer teachers. *Nurse Education in Practice, 11*(2), 141–145.

McLane, J. B. (1987). Interaction, context and the zone of proximal development. In M. Hickmann (Eds.). *Social and functional approaches to language and thought* (pp. 267–285). Orlando: Academic Press.

Miquel, E. (2006). Maestros que trabajando juntos aprenden. *Aula de innovación educativa, 153–154*, 33–36.

Monereo, C. (Ed.), Badia, A., Domènech, M., Escofet, A., Fuentes, M. Rodríguez, J. L., Tirado, F. J. & Vayreda, A. (2005). *Internet y competencias básicas: Aprender a colaborar, a comunicarse, a participar, a aprender*. Barcelona: Graó.

Monereo, C., Pozo, J. I. & Castelló, M. (2001). La enseñanza de estrategias de aprendizaje en el contexto escolar. In C. Coll, J. Palacios & Á. Marchesi (Eds.). *Desarrollo psicológico y educación. 2. Psicologia de la educación escolar* (pp. 235–258). Madrid: Alianza.

Monimó, J. M., Sigalés, C. & Meneses, J. (2008). *La escuela en la sociedad red. Internet en la educación primaria y secundaria*. Barcelona: Ariel.

Montante, J. M., Nazar, N. & Bee, M. (2013). Learning by teaching: Service learning in anatomy. *Journal Online by the Federation of American Societies for Experimental Biology, 27*, 961.4.

Morin, E. (2001). *La mente bien ordenada: Repensar la reforma, reformar el pensamiento*. Barcelona: Seix Barral.

Mosca, A. & Santiviago, C. (2010). *Tutorías de estudiantes, Tutorías entre pares*. Montevideo: Universidad de la República-Progresa.

Nestojko, J. F., Bui, D. C., Kornell, N. & Bjork, E. L. (2014). Expecting to teach enhances learning and organization of knowledge in free recall of text passages. *Memory and Cognition, 42*, 1038–1048.

Nonaka, I. & Takeuchi, H. (1995). *The knowledge-creating company*. New York: Oxford University Press.

November, A. (2012). *Who owns the learning? Preparing students for success in the digital world*. Bloomington, IN: Solution Tree Press.

O'Donnell, A. & King, A. (Eds.) (1999). *Cognitive perspectives on peer learning*. Mahwah, NJ: Lawrence Erlbaum Associates, Inc.

O'Donnell, A. & Topping, K. J. (1998). Peers assessing peers: Possibilities and problems. In K. J. Topping & S. Ehly (Eds.). *Peer-assisted learning* (pp. 255–278). Mahwah, NJ: Lawrence Erlbaum Associates.

Ofcom (2014). *Children and parents: Media use and attitudes report*. London: Ofcom.

OFSTED (2001). *Family learning. A survey of good practice*. London: HMSO.

Okita, S. & Schwartz D. (2013). Learning by teaching human pupils and teachable agents: The importance of recursive feedback. *Journal of the Learning Sciences, 22*(3), 375–412.

Palincsar, A. & Brown, A. (2009). Interactive teaching to promote independent learning from text. In D. Lapp & D. Fisher (Eds.). *Essential readings on comprehension* (pp. 771–777). Newark, DE: International Reading Association.

Palincsar, A. & Brown, A. (1984). Reciprocal teaching of comprehension-fostering and metacognitive strategies. *Cognition and Instruction, 1*, 117–175.

Perrenoud, P. (2012). *Cuando la escuela pretende preparar para la vida. ¿Desarrollar competencias o enseñar otros saberes?* Barcelona: Graó.

Perrenoud, P. (2004). *Desarrollar la práctica reflexiva en el oficio de enseñar.* Barcelona: Graó.

Perrenoud, P. (2001). The key to social fields: Competencies of an autonomous actor. In D. S. Rychen & L. H. Salganik (Eds.). *Defining and selecting key competences* (pp. 121–150). Göttingen: Hogrefe & Huber.

Pinker, S. (1997). *How the mind works.* New York: Norton.

Ploetzner R., Dillenbourg P., Praier M. & Traum D. (1999). Learning by explaining to oneself and to others. In P. Dillenbourg (Ed.). *Collaborative-learning: Cognitive and computational approaches* (pp. 103–121). Oxford: Elsevier.

Pozo, J. I. (2006). La nueva cultura del aprendizaje en la sociedad del conocimiento. In J. I. Pozo, N. Scheuer, M. del P. Pérez Echeverría, M. Mateos, E. Martín & M. de la Cruz (Eds.). *Nuevas formas de pensar la enseñanza y el aprendizaje* (pp. 29–53). Barcelona: Graó.

Pozo, J. I. (2001). *Humana mente: El mundo, la conciencia y la carne.* Madrid: Morata.

Pozo, J. I. (1996). *Aprendices y maestros.* Madrid: Alianza Editorial.

Pozo, J. I., Monereo, C. & Castelló, M. (2001). El uso estratégico del conocimiento. In C. Coll, J. Palacios & A. Marchesi (Eds.). *Desarrollo psicológico y educación. 2. Psicología de la educación escolar* (pp. 211–234). Madrid: Alianza Editorial.

Pozo, J. I., Scheuer, N. Mateos, M. & Pérez Echeverría, M. P. (2006). Las teorías implícitas sobre el aprendizaje y la enseñanza. In J. I. Pozo, N. Scheuer, M. del P. Pérez Echeverría, M. Mateos, E. Martín & M. de la Cruz (Eds.). *Nuevas formas de pensar la enseñanza y el aprendizaje* (pp. 95–134). Barcelona: Graó.

Pozo, J. I., Scheuer, N., Pérez Echeverría, M. del P., Mateos, M., Martín E. & de la Cruz, M. (Eds.). (2006). *Nuevas formas de pensar la enseñanza y el aprendizaje.* Barcelona: Graó.

Presnky, M. (2010). *Teaching digital natives: Partnering for real learning.* Thousand Oaks, CA: Corwin.

Puig, J. M. (Eds.) (2009). *Aprendizaje servicio (ApS). Educación y compromiso cívico.* Barcelona: Graó.

Pujolàs, P. (2008). *El aprendizaje cooperativo.* Barcelona: Graó.

Reig, D. (2012). Educación social autónoma abierta. In R. Díaz, J. Freire, B. Lamb, J. Martín et al. (Eds.). *Educación expandida* (pp. 208–226). Sevilla: Zemos 98.

Reynolds, C. M. (Ed.) (1989). *Knowledge base for the beginning teacher.* Oxford: Pergamon.

Rhodes, C., Sokes, M. & Hampton, G. (2004). *A practical guide to mentoring, coaching and peer-networking. Teacher professional development in schools and colleges.* London: RoutledgeFalmer.

Rogoff, B. (1990). *Apprenticeship in thinking: Cognitive development in social context.* New York: Oxford University Press.

Roscoe, R. (2014). Self-monitoring and knowledge-building in learning by teaching. *Instructional Science, 42*, 327–351.

Roscoe, R. & Chi, M. (2007). Understanding tutor learning: Knowledge-building and knowledge-telling in peer tutors' explanations and questions. *Review of Educational Research, 77*(4), 534–574.

Rosenshine, B. & Meister, C. (1994). Reciprocal teaching: A review of the research. *Review of Educational Research, 64*(4), 479–530.

Rué, J. (1998). El aula: Un espacio para la cooperación. In C. Mir (Ed.). *Cooperar en la escuela. La responsabilidad de educar para la democracia* (pp. 17–50). Barcelona: Graó.

Ruiz-Bikandi, U. & Camps, A. (2007). Corrientes en investigación educativa y formación del profesorado: Una visión de conjunto. *Cultura y Educación, 19*(2), 105–122.

Rytivaara, A., & Kershner, R. (2012). Co-teaching as a context for teachers' professional learning and joint knowledge construction. *Teaching and Teacher Education, 28*, 999–1008.

Sanmartí, N. (2007). *Evaluar para aprender*. Barcelona: Graó.

Santos Guerra, M. A. (2012). Adelantarse al futuro: Agrupamientos del alumnado. In B. Jaruata & F. Imbernón (Eds.). *Pensando en el futuro de la educación. Una nueva escuela para el siglo XXII* (pp. 83–100). Barcelona: Graó.

Santos Guerra, M. A. (2001). *La escuela que aprende*. Madrid: Morata.

Sapon-Shavin, M. (1999). *Because we can change the world. A practical guide to building cooperative, inclusive classroom communities*. Needham Heights, MA: Allyn & Bacon.

Scheuer, N., Pozo, J. I., Pérez Echeverría, M. P., Mateos, M. M., Ortega, E. M. & de la Cruz, M. (2006). *Nuevas formas de pensar la enseñanza y el aprendizaje : las concepciones de profesores y alumnos*. Barcelona: Graó.

Schön, D. A. (1991). *The reflective practitioner: How professionals think in action*. Aldershot: Avebury.

Sharan, Y. (2010). Cooperative learning for academic and social gains: Valued pedagogy, problematic practice. *European Journal of Education, 45*(2), 300–313.

Sharan, Y. & Sharan, S. (1994). Group investigation in the cooperative classroom. In S. Sharan (Ed.). *Handbook of cooperative learning methods*. London: Praeger.

Siemens, G. (2005). Connectivism: A learning theory for the digital age. *International Journal of Instructional Technology and Distance Learning, 2*(1), 3–10.

Silberman, M. (1996). The use of pairs in cooperative learning. *Cooperative Learning and College Teaching, 7*(1), 2–12.

Sinclair, J. & Coulthard, M. (1975). *Towards an analysis of discourse: The English used by teachers and pupils*. London: Oxford University Press.

Slavin, R. (1996). Research for the future. Research on cooperative learning and achievement: What we know, what we need to know. *Contemporary Educational Psychology, 21*, 43–69.

Slavin, R. (1995). *Cooperative learning*. Boston, MA: Allyn & Bacon.

Slavin, R. (1978). *Using student team learning*. Baltimore: Center for Social Organization of Schools. The Johns Hopkins University.

Soler, R. (2003). *Mentoring. Estrategia de desarrollo de Recursos Humanos*. Barcelona: Gestión 2000.

Springer, L., Stanne, E. & Donovan, S. (1999). Effects of small-group learning on undergraduates in science, mathematics, engineering, and technology: A meta-analysis. *Review of Educational Research, 69*, 21–51.

Stainback, S. & Stainback, W. (1999). *Curriculum consideration in inclusive classrooms*. Baltimore: Paul H. Brookes.

Stake, R. E. (2004). *Standards-based and responsive evaluation*. Thousand Oaks, CA: Sage Publications.

Tang, T., Hernandez, E. & Adams, B. (2004). Learning by teaching: A peer-teaching model for diversity training in medical school. *Teaching and Learning in Medicine, 16*(1), 60–63.

Thomas, D. & Seely Brown, J. (2011). *A new culture of learning: Cultivating the imagination for a world of constant change*. London: Kogan Page.

Thurston, A., Duran, D., Cunningham, E., Blanch, S., & Topping, K. (2009). International online reciprocal peer tutoring to promote modern language development in primary schools. *Computers and Education, 53*, 462–472. Also in Spanish as: Tutoría entre iguales recíproca y virtual para la mejora de habilidades lingüísticas en español e inglés. (2010). *Infancia y Aprendizaje, 33*(2), 209–222.

Tomasello, M. (2009). *Why we cooperate*. Cambridge, MA: MIT Press.

Tomasello, M., Hare, H., Lehmann, H. & Call, J. (2007). The cooperative eye hypothesis. *Journal of Human Evolution, 52*(3), 314–320.

Topping, K. J. (2015). Peer tutoring: Old method, new developments. *Infancia y Aprendizaje*, *38*(1), 1–29.

Topping, K. J. (2010). Methodological quandaries in studying process and outcomes in peer assessment. *Learning and Instruction*, *20*(4), 339–343.

Topping, K. J. (2005). Trends in peer learning. *Educational Psychology*, *25*(6), 631–645.

Topping, K. J. (2000). *Tutoring by peers, family and volunteers*. Geneva: UNESCO.

Topping, K. J. (1998). Peer assessment between students in college and university. *Review of Educational Research*, *68*(3), 249–276.

Topping, K. J. (1996). *Effective peer tutoring in further and higher education*. Birmingham: SEDA Paper.

Topping, K. J., Buchs, C., Duran, D. & Van Keer, H. (2017). *Effective peer learning: From principles to practical implementation*. London: Routledge.

Topping, K. J., Dehkinet, R., Blanch, S., Corcelles, M. & Duran, D. (2013). Paradoxical effects of feedback in international online reciprocal peer tutoring. *Computers & Education*, *61*, 225–231.

Topping, K. J., Duran, D. & Van Keer, H. (2016). *Using peer tutoring to improve reading skills. A practical guide for teachers*. London: Routledge.

Topping, K. J. & Ehly, S. (eds.). (1998). *Peer-assisted learning*. Mahwah, NJ: Lawrence Erlbaum Associates.

UNESCO (1996). *Learning: The treasure within. Report to UNESCO of the International Commission on Education for the Twenty-first Century*. Paris: UNESCO.

Valdebenito, V. & Duran, D. (2015). Formas de interacción implicadas en la promoción de estrategias de comprensión lectora a través de un programa de tutoría entre iguales. *Revista Latinoamericana de Psicología*, *47*(2), 75–85.

Van der Klift, E. & Kunc, N. (1994). Beyond benevolence: Friendship and the politics of help. In J. Thousand, R. Villa & A. Nevin (Eds.). *Creativity and collaborative learning* (pp. 391–402). Baltimore, MA: Brookes.

Varas, M. & Zariquiey, F. (2011). Técnicas formales e informales de aprendizaje cooperativo. In J. C. Torrego (Ed.). *Alumnos con altas capacidades y aprendizaje cooperativo* (pp. 505–560). Madrid: Fundación SM.

Villa, R. A., Thousand, J. S. & Nevin, A. I. (2010). *Collaborating with students in instruction and decision making. The untapped resource*. Thousand Oaks, CA: Corwin.

Villa, R. A., Thousand, J. S. & Nevin, A. I. (2008). *A guide to co-teaching: Practical strategies for facilitating student learning*. Thousand Oaks, CA: Corwin.

Vinagre, M. (2010). *Teoría y práctica del aprendizaje colaborativo asistido por ordenador*. Madrid: Síntesis.

Vygotsky, L. S. (1978). *Mind in society: The development of higher psychological processes*. Cambridge, MA: Harvard University Press.

Walberg, H. & Paik, S. (2000). *Effective educational practices*. Geneva: International Academy of Education.

Warneken, F., Chen. F. & Tomasello, M. (2006). Cooperative activities in young children and chimpanzees. *Child Development*, *3*, 640–663.

Webb, N. M. (1989). Peer interaction and learning in small groups. *International Journal of Educational Research*, *13*, 21–39.

Wells, G. (1999). *Dialogic inquiry*. Cambridge: Press Syndicate of the University of Cambridge.

Wertsch, J. V. (1985). *Vygotsky and the social formation of mind*. Cambridge, MA: Harvard University Press.

Whitman, N. (1988). *Peer teaching: To teach is to learn twice*. ASHE-ERIC Higher Education Report, 4. Washington: Association for the Study of Higher Education.

Wood, D. J., Bruner, J. S. & Ross, G. (1976). The role of tutoring in problem solving. *Journal of Child Psychology and Psychiatry*, *17*, 89–100.

Zajonc, R. B. (1966). *Social psychology: An experimental approach*. Belmont, CA: Wadsworth.

Index